JESUS:
A Friend of Mine

PERSONAL ENCOUNTERS WITH JESUS AS TOLD BY THE PEOPLE HE TOUCHED

John C. Westervelt

PENBROOKE
PUBLISHING

ISBN 1-889116-16-5

Printed in the United States of America

First U.S. Edition

Design by
Paragon Communications Group, Inc., Tulsa, Oklahoma

Published by
PENBROOKE PUBLISHING
Tulsa, Oklahoma

Introduction

*W*ithin the pages of this book are the stories of thirty-two people who met Jesus. Some of them are young, and some of them are old. Some are rich, and some are poor. Some of them are well documented by the gospel writers; others received just a few lines. But as you read, you will come to know the rest of their story, for just like you and me, they each have a story to tell.

Yes, my imagination and God's help were required to pick up where the gospel writers left off. I believe, however, that as you read their stories they will become more real to you, and just as they met Jesus, you will meet Him too.

John C. Westervelt

Contents

Jesus' Final Journey to Jerusalem

Many Years Later

Acknowledgement

Three Special Young Women

My daughter, Mary Kim Gray, listened to my first spoken stories, encouraged me to write them, and edited each one.

Deanne Crimmel, a seminary graduate and tough, professional editor, reworked each story twice and sometimes more.

Jan Weinheimer, editor of my local church paper, encouraged me to keep writing each month, until thirty-two stories had been published in the *Asbury Tidings.*

Mary Kim, Deanne, and Jan, my love for you deepened as we labored together for thirty-two months to tell the stories of those who met Jesus.

Martha: The Homemaker

*M*y name is Martha. I live in Bethany, a village two miles east of Jerusalem, with my brother Lazarus and my younger sister Mary. Lazarus' good friend Jesus, a Galilean, often visited in our home when He was in Jerusalem. Ever since His first visit, Mary and I have felt as if we were His good friends, too.

It all started when one early spring day Lazarus returned from business in Jerusalem to say that he had seen Jesus and had invited Him to come to lunch the following day. Since I pride myself on being a good cook and homemaker, my mind immediately went to work on the next day's menu. For some time I had wanted to prepare a nourishing meal for Jesus, as I had remembered Lazarus telling me about the disciples urging Jesus to eat when He had not. Finally, my chance had come.

Of course, the house needed to be cleaned and the food bought before I could even begin. So I worked late into the night sweeping the floors and filling the olive oil lamps. It was well past midnight when I laid down in the comfort of my bed. The crowing of the rooster just before dawn startled me and I awoke. Then I jumped out of bed to prepare myself for my trip to the market. I hurried from shop to shop so I would be home in time to start the fire to slowly cook the mutton. A lunch could easily become a feast for such a special friend.

When I returned home, Mary had gone out into the countryside to gather wildflowers to place in vases to color and sweeten the rooms. So I spent most of the morning alone in the kitchen doing all the preparation. By this time my feet and back were aching. Out the window I could see the shortening shadows signifying noon. Just as Mary was coming through the back door with a handful of wildflowers, Lazarus called out, "Jesus is here!"

Quickly, I wiped off my hands and walked to the living area where Jesus was greeting Mary with a friendly hug. I interrupted by saying, "I'm so glad you were able to come. Please have a seat in the living room and visit while I finish getting the food ready. I think it is just about done. Will you please excuse me?"

Hurriedly I stepped into the kitchen to test the meat. The mutton was just right and the vegetables were ready to be dished up for serving. I needed someone to get the wine from storage and the dishes to the table. In my frustration, I walked into the living room and said, "Jesus, doesn't it seem unfair to you that my sister just sits here while I do all the work? Tell her to come and help me!"

"Martha, my dear Martha, you are so upset over all these details. There is really only one thing worth being concerned about, and Mary has discovered it. I won't take it away from her."

I was a little taken back by Jesus' response, and I could feel my face flush as I returned to the kitchen. But despite my feelings, I hurried to get the mutton on the platter, the vegetables in the bowls, and the wine from storage.

Once we were all seated around the table, Lazarus kept asking Jesus questions like, "You said you must die and then return to life. How is such a thing possible?"

His only reply was, "You shall see."

I didn't break into the conversation because I was busy getting more bread and wine, or maybe I was pouting with a smile. As the bowls were emptied, I carried them into the kitchen. Standing alone cleaning the dishes, I wondered, "Does Jesus love Mary more than me? Maybe she is prettier." When I had asked my mother about it as a thirteen-year-old, she had told me, "Just because you are big boned like I am doesn't mean you aren't pretty. You have a sweet face, and besides, true beauty is from the heart." I felt good about myself then, but not now.

I was finished with the dishes and was wiping down the water basin when I sensed someone approach me from behind.

"Martha. Martha."

I continued looking out the window while slowly wiping my hands. My eyes welled up with tears until they were so full that they began to roll down my cheeks and drip silently into the basin. Because I am the strong one in the family, I didn't say a word. Then Jesus touched me on the shoulders and gently turned me around. I felt so ashamed that I covered my face with both hands, but Jesus' long arms reached around me and pulled me close. It was then that I really began to cry. He continued to hold me with His left hand and stroked my hair with His right. I moved my wet hands from my face and laid my head and the palms of both my hands on His chest. Then with a comforting sigh, Jesus said, "I love no one more than you, Martha. I want Mary to be Mary, and Martha to be Martha."

Based on Luke 10:38-42; John 4:31-34.

Mary of Bethany: The Dreamer

*M*y name is Mary. I live in Bethany with my older sister and brother, Martha and Lazarus. I remember when we moved to Bethany from Jerusalem. My father's business as a trader had prospered, so he was able to build us a larger home in the country. I was only four when all of our belongings were loaded on carts behind donkeys for the two mile journey. Ever since, I have loved being in the countryside of this small village because I can gather wildflowers in the fields nearby.

Martha has loved to cook since early childhood. She was always beside my mother anytime she was in the kitchen. I, on the other hand, was on my father's lap as a child and sitting at his feet when older, listening to him tell stories about the prophets and kings and queens. My favorite was the story about Queen Esther. As a child I often would tie a rolled scarf around my head pretending it was a crown and that I was a queen, just like Esther.

Four years ago, on my twelfth birthday, my father gave me an alabaster jar filled with spikenard, one of the most expensive cream perfumes you can buy. He said the spikenard was a gift to be used on my wedding night in a few more years.

Lazarus' work with my father often took him to the cities of Galilee where he sometimes stayed in Capernaum. It was in the synagogue in Capernaum that Lazarus first met Jesus, and they are now best of friends.

Once I overheard my father telling a business friend how proud he was of his children, "Lazarus has always been such good help in the business, and Martha in the home. Mary is the artistic one who fills the house with flowers and laughter." I shall never forget that my father loved me just the way I was.

Life has never been quite the same since the night that our neighbor came to our door carrying an olive oil lamp and told us our parents had been killed by robbers for the goods they were carrying. Oh, how I wish my father and mother had not taken that trip to Jericho two years ago.

Martha, though only eighteen at the time, was so strong. It hasn't been easy, but she and Lazarus have managed to keep us together as a family in the house that my father built. Sometimes before I go to bed, I retrieve my precious gift of spikenard from the bottom of the chest at the foot of my bed and hug it close to me remembering the love of my father and mother.

Jesus came to our house as Lazarus' friend for the funeral of my father and mother. He left as a good friend of Martha and me as well. Lazarus had told me how busy Jesus was as He walked the countryside telling the people about God, still He continued to find time to visit Martha and me.

Not long ago, Lazarus became suddenly ill. Martha and I sent a message to Jesus because He had always been here when we needed Him. But Lazarus died before Jesus could come. I questioned, "Jehovah, why? First my father and mother and now Lazarus. It just doesn't seem fair."

Jesus eventually did arrive, but it was four days too late. When Martha went out to meet Him, she returned only to say, "He is here and wants to see you."

So I went at once. When I saw Him, I immediately fell down at His feet weeping and saying, "If You had been here, my brother would still be alive."

Tears came to Jesus' eyes as He asked, "Where is he buried?"

When I told Him, He said, "Come, let's get Martha and go to the tomb."

As we approached the tomb, mourners lined the walkway. Upon reaching the sepulcher Jesus shouted, "Lazarus, come forth!" Before our very eyes, the stone rolled away, and Lazarus was returned alive and well to Martha and me. I was happy and sad all at the same time, and I didn't know whether to laugh or cry. If I hadn't seen it myself, I don't know if I would have believed it.

Several weeks later, six days before Passover, Jesus came to our house for a banquet. This was a celebration of Jesus' healing ministry. Andrew told Lazarus that Jesus had said that He would die then rise again from the dead.

Even though I knew that it was possible for someone to be raised from the dead, I felt a deep sadness settle over me. During the banquet I went to my room and dug down to the bottom of my wooden chest and pulled out my jar of spikenard. I thought about my wedding night. It would be a special moment between the two of us when we would open the jar together. Then I thought about my friend Jesus and I removed the snug fitting lid to smell the sweet perfume.

As I entered the living room, Jesus looked away from the conversations, and His kind eyes locked on mine. I moved to where He lounged, knelt beside Him, and began to rub the spikenard on His feet. I slowly rubbed all my perfume into the tough skin of the feet of this One who had walked so far for others. Thinking of His dying, I began to cry. Salty tears fell on Jesus' feet, so I grasped a handful of my hair and blotted up the tear stains. No one said a word as I put the lid back on the jar then held it close to me as I slowly walked out of the room.

Judas broke the silence, "Why was this ointment not sold for three hundred denarii and given to the poor?"

As I reached the hall I could hear the quiet but persistent words of Jesus, "Let her alone. She did it in preparation for my burial. She has used her spikenard, intended by her father for her most joyous occasion, as a gift to me for my grievous one. The poor you have with you always, but you do not always have me."

Based on John 11 and 12.

Lazarus: Jesus' Good Friend

*M*y name is Lazarus. I live in Bethany with my two sisters, Martha, who is two years older, and Mary, who is two years younger. As a child I attended school at the synagogue. I studied hard because my parents believed that education was important. My mother schooled Martha and Mary at home. When I came home from class, I would share parts of the day's lessons with my sisters.

As an older boy, I worked in the family trading business. At age fifteen, I began to travel to the cities of Galilee where my father was expanding the business outside of Judea. Capernaum was chosen as my home away from home since it is a trading center. Every two months I would make the one hundred mile journey home to Bethany where I would stay for two weeks before returning to Galilee.

In Bethany I had spent time in the synagogue reading the scrolls just for the pleasure of it, so it was natural for me to go to the synagogue in Capernaum. A teacher from Nazareth named Jesus had moved to Capernaum and would frequently teach in the synagogue. I had just been seated one evening when a friendly man approached me and said, "My name is Andrew. May I sit beside you?."

"Yes. My name is Lazarus. My home is in Bethany, but I am in Capernaum most of the time to expand my family's trading business."

Jesus read from the prophets and then told stories that illustrated God's instructions for us. Jesus was warm and friendly but, at the same time, so incisive in His explanation of the Scriptures. I could not help but admire Him. After Jesus had finished speaking, Andrew asked, "Would you like to meet Jesus?"

"Oh, I would like that very much."

We waited together until the group clustered about Jesus began to thin out before Andrew approached Jesus and said, "This is Lazarus from Bethany. He spends time in Capernaum as a trader in his family's business."

"Welcome to Capernaum, Lazarus. Come back to our meetings anytime you can. There is so much to learn about God and His Word."

Each time Jesus spoke, I would stay around afterwards to talk with Him. He clarified many questions I had about the Scriptures. Eventually it was time for Him to move on to other cities, so I invited Jesus to visit Martha, Mary, and me in Bethany whenever He was in Jerusalem.

I was in Bethany when my sisters and I received the message of the death of our parents at the hands of robbers on the road to Jericho. This sad news spread across Bethany and into Jerusalem. Jesus was staying in Jerusalem at the time and graciously came to the funeral. He was an immense comfort to all three of us and became a very close friend of the family.

In the meantime, I hired a man to take over the accounts in Galilee so I could call on my father's customers in Judea. I was glad that Jesus had come to Judea to continue the ministry which He had started in Galilee. He had shared with me privately that He hoped the Jewish people of Jerusalem would accept Him as their Messiah.

I had enjoyed good health all of my life, so I was not prepared when sickness struck me suddenly. I can recall the onset of a high fever followed by the peace of being with the Lord. Then all at once I heard the voice of Jesus calling to me, "Lazarus, come forth!"

I was totally disoriented when I heard His voice and didn't know where I was. I could tell I was in a dark, dank place which I finally decided was my family's tomb. My hands and feet were wrapped in burial cloths and my face covered with a burial napkin. I felt a little faint, but I stood up and started walking towards Jesus' voice. It wasn't long until the darkness turned to light as someone pulled off the napkin and began to unwind the burial cloths. At first the shapes of people were blurred, but after a few moments I could see that Martha and Mary were the ones freeing me from my death wraps. Behind them stood my powerful friend, Jesus. His face was wet with tears.

Several weeks later, six days before Passover, Jesus came to our house for a banquet. Andrew, the disciple who first introduced me to Him, said, "Jesus told us that He must be killed and then be raised from the dead."

"How could anyone do such a dreadful thing to a man who has been so good to others?"

"John thinks Jesus' death and resurrection are required to save each of us from our sins because Jesus once said, 'Unless a grain of wheat falls into the earth and dies, it remains alone; but if it dies it bears much fruit.'"

What Andrew said ended up being true, and Jesus was killed soon after. His death was a gruesome sight. The miracle of His resurrection made believers of many who had questioned Jesus' claim that He was the Son of God. My family and I were not surprised by Jesus' being raised from the dead since we had already experienced my own resurrection and had concluded that Jesus was indeed the Son of God.

During the weeks that followed His death, Martha talked with Mary and me saying, "We must do our part to honor Jesus. Let's make our home available so that believers may have a place to meet and worship Him." And so we did.

From then until now, I have never again feared death and know that when my day comes I will face it with full confidence knowing that to be absent from my body is to be present with the Lord.

Based on John 11 and 12; Matthew 18:20.

Bernice:
Why Does She Care So?

*M*y name is John. My work as a trader had taken me from my home in Caesarea Maritima to Jerusalem, sixty miles southeast. I had spent the week at an inn while buying and selling. On Friday I awoke to the smell of porridge being cooked in the kitchen. The innkeeper there served a hearty breakfast. When I sat down at the table and looked out the doorway, I could see people swarming up the narrow street, all going the same direction. As I began to eat, I asked the innkeeper, "Where is everyone going?"

"Have you not heard? There are to be three crucifixions today."

I was not sure I had the stomach for such a thing, but with time on my hands I followed the crowd to about a hundred feet from the top of the hill. I stopped, but the noisy crowd pressed in close to yell jeers and shake their fists at the men who were to be crucified.

A young woman who was alone stopped next to me. She appeared to be in her early thirties, just a few years younger than my own daughter. Her eyes were fixed on the center cross. I studied her beautiful face. The lock of hair showing from under her hood was coal black as were her eyes. Her smooth complexion radiated beauty in itself. Her features were delicate. I wished she would smile. But she didn't. Her face was set in a grimace that pressed her lips together so tightly that they had lost their color. I was struck by the vise grip of her hand where she held the hood covering her head and part of her face. Her knuckles were white.

As a grandfather I might view a crucifixion once in my lifetime, but why would a young woman put herself through such an ordeal? I sensed a kinship with this one, like my feelings for family. I needed to know more.

"Shalom, my name is John."

Her eyes moved to meet mine, "Shalom, I am Bernice."

There was silence for awhile as she looked at the ground, then she looked up. Her eyes welled up with tears, "How can they do this to Him? It is so unfair."

Her gaze returned to the One being laid on the center cross. Who could He be that she cared so much? Those around her taunted Him, "You saved others. Now save yourself!"

As I glanced back at the center cross, I could see a hammer, held by a soldier, being raised above the hand tied to the wooden beam. For the first time, the crowd turned deathly still. Next there was a ring of metal against metal as the hammer met the nail. Every muscle of the One laid on the cross quivered in pain. I looked away.

My new-found companion began to cry uncontrollably. Almost instinctively I took her into my arms, as if she were my own daughter. All of her small body shook with her sobs. I wondered if she could breathe. My gentle hold firmed as tears flowed down my cheeks too. Many minutes passed before her regular breathing returned. With my right arm still holding her, we turned to look up the hill. The cross now stood erect.

"Bernice, who is He?"

"He is my brother."

I caught my breath. My insides drew taut. Her eyes were wet, but she seemed composed.

"I want to go to the foot of the cross, but my mother, who is there now, instructed me not to come here. I have never disobeyed her before."

"I have a daughter like you. Would you like for me to take you to your home?"

"No, Jesus would want me to stay until He dies."

How could she hold up to such a gruesome sight. This cruel death would be slow. The least I could do was wait with her.

"Are there brothers and sisters besides you and Jesus?"

"I have four brothers and two sisters, all younger than I. Jesus and I have always been close, not just because we are the oldest, but because we share the same spirit."

"Did you play together as children?"

"Yes, Jesus would save the wood scraps and carve them into blocks for me. He kept them in a basket under His carpenter's bench. He even invented a special game that only He and I played called Jerusalem's Temple. He would help me lay out the temple buildings and the walls with the blocks. He had learned the dimensions at school. I wish I could have gone to school at the synagogue with Him, but I am just a girl."

"When my father died, not long after the birth of Simon, I was needed to help with the children, so I never married. As a teenager and, yes, even in my twenties, I would ask with a smile, 'Jesus, can we play Jerusalem's Temple?' With just the two of us in the shop, I would place the blocks while we talked."

"Do you still play your game?"

"Not very often. During the last three years, He has been traveling to other towns with His disciples."

While we were talking, dark clouds had begun to gather. Jagged lightning streaked from the clouds to the earth and was followed by deafening thunder. A cold rain began to spit into my face. Bernice gripped my hand as she moved closer to the cross.

Jesus appeared to be in excruciating pain. He had to push Himself up on the cross just to get enough breath to speak. In the crowd was an older woman to whom He spoke saying, "Woman, behold your son."

With more labor to breathe, He said to the man next to the woman, "Behold your mother."

Bernice's breathing was as troubled as Jesus' when He looked at her and said, "Someday we shall be together in Jerusalem's Temple."

His body strained one last time for air, then He cried out, "It is finished!"

At His words, Bernice loosened her grip on my hand. Her lips, which had been white, were now red. Color returned to her knuckles. As she relaxed her hold on her hood, it fell to her shoulders. A gentle wind blew through her hair adding to her beauty. I then knew that Jesus would keep His promise and that someday they would be together again in Jerusalem's Temple.

Based on Mark 6:3; John 19:26-27.

Mary of Nazareth: In Service at the Wedding Party

I am known as Grandpa John because that is what Anne has always called me. I own a basket making business in Cana of Galilee where we enjoy a good supply of reeds. My baskets are sold in Cana and throughout the surrounding area. Traders travel the thirty miles from Caesarea Maritima, the Roman port city, to buy my baskets. They also bring with them ribbons of cloth cut from fine cotton. Last week I purchased some and am now adding it to five of the flower baskets for the wedding party of Anne and Joel at his father's house. Joel's grandfather and father are my good friends, so I am looking forward to becoming part of their family.

Soon the ribbons were all tied, so I wrapped the baskets in a small piece of fish net, swung the bundle across my shoulder, and headed for Joel's house to meet his mother, Edna. She would add the flowers and distribute the baskets throughout the house and in the garden to add a decorative touch to the festivities.

As I sauntered down the hillside near Joel's house, I thought about my granddaughter. We have always been close. When she was just a little girl, I remember holding her on my lap. When she became a little older, I remember taking her by the hand and showing her the flowers along the side of my house.

When she became old enough to learn to weave baskets on her own, I remember teaching her how to make the simpler designs. Once she reached the age of eligibility, however, she began to think more about marriage than baskets. When I saw how well she and Joel always got along together, I thought they might marry someday. As it turned out, I was right, and now she is the beautiful bride of one of the finest young men in our town.

As I approached the doorway, Anne caught a glimpse of me and excused herself from the group she was talking with then headed towards me. In her hair was a flower she had picked from my yard and on her face was a radiant smile. When she reached me, she greeted me with a kiss. Joel was right behind her and gave her a quick kiss on the neck then told me that his mother had been watching for me at the gate. Since I had slipped in the back way, I had missed her altogether.

When Edna entered the room and saw me, she looked relieved and quickly escorted me to the alcove where she had all of the flowers. After I told her where I had put the baskets, she sent a servant to get them. As we stood there, I asked Edna, "Who are those two attractive women across the way that I have not seen before?"

"They are Mary from Nazareth and her daughter Bernice. I hired them to help me with the wedding party."

I couldn't take my eyes off of Mary. She stood out for she was more beautiful than any other guest. Her features were delicate. Her hair was coal-black as were her eyes, and her smooth complexion radiated beauty. From where I stood, she could be the sister, rather than the mother, of her equally beautiful daughter. Wanting to know more, I moved to where Mary stood to introduce myself.

"I am John, grandfather of the bride. Do you and your daughter often help with wedding parties?"

"Yes, ever since my husband died."

"Your daughter is so beautiful. Has she not married?"

"Bernice, my next born after Jesus, helped me raise her four younger brothers and two sisters. As a result, she wasn't really available for marriage when her time should have come."

"Possibly you shouldn't give up hope so soon for one so pretty."

"I suppose only Jehovah knows what the future may hold."

"Edna told me she invited your son, Jesus, and His disciples. Both she and Anne have known Jesus as a friend ever since He first spoke in our synagogue."

Suddenly one of the servants interrupted our conversation to say, "Mary, we have run out of wine! We must not embarrass Joel. He didn't know how much would be needed."

Mary turned back to me, "Come, let's find Jesus."

So I followed Mary to the alcove where Jesus was telling stories to those gathered around Him. Jesus looked relaxed sitting on a bench in front of the window. The bright daylight lit the faces of the attentive listeners who appeared to be enjoying the storyteller. There was something about Jesus that made me like Him right away. Mary called her son aside to say, "They have no more wine."

Jesus said, "I can't help you now. It isn't yet my time for miracles." Still He immediately spoke to the servants saying, "Fill the six stone waterpots with water."

I glanced at the waterpots, estimating that each pot would hold twenty-five to thirty gallons. Then I heard Mary tell the servants, "Do whatever He says."

When the servants finished, Mary's son said, "Dip some out and take it to the steward."

Mary and I followed the servant to where the steward drank from the cup. I was amazed when the steward called Joel over and said to him, "Every man serves the good wine first; and when men have drunk freely, then the poor wine; but you have kept the best for the last."

I was surprised to hear that the water had been changed to wine, so when Mary and I stood alone again, I asked, "Was the wine from water some sort of a miracle?"

"What we saw we must believe."

"Has he performed miracles before?"

"No, this is the first."

"Can you explain it?"

"I can't. But let me share some things I have treasured in my heart for many years. Jesus' birth was miraculous in itself. Then, when Joseph and I took Jesus as a baby to the temple in Jerusalem to present Him to the Lord, we were met by an old man, Simeon, who told us that Jesus would be the Savior of the world and that a sword would pierce my soul. When Jesus was twelve, He remained in Jerusalem when our family was returning home after a journey there for the Passover celebration. When Joseph and I went back, we found Him in the temple, sitting among the teachers, listening to them and asking them questions. All who heard Him were amazed at His understanding and His answers."

"Did He willingly go home with you?"

"Yes, He returned to the carpentry shop where He worked diligently, first with his father, then later alone, until just a few months ago when He gathered around Him twelve disciples and began teaching the people about God."

"You must feel sad in a way to no longer have your oldest son with you, but as a good Jewish mother you seem willing to release Him for the Lord's work."

"Yes, I feel a sadness but at the same time much joy, for from the time I became pregnant with Jesus until today I have known that He was set apart by Jehovah for a very special purpose and I wait with a certain expectation to see the plan unfold."

Based on John 2:1-11; Luke 2:28-35,41-52.

Anna: The Prophetess Who Saw the Messiah

*M*y name is Anna. During my youth I lived in Kanah, which is eight miles southeast of Tyre or twenty-five miles northwest of the Sea of Galilee. My father Phanuel and I were always very close. Oftentimes he would take me to the synagogue when no one else was there and read to me about the Jewish prophets from the scrolls. One story was about Kanah and described a leader, named Joshua, who had divided the remaining promised land into seven portions. He then cast lots to determine which tribe would get which section. The fifth lot, which included the town of Kanah, fell to the tribe of Asher, which is my family's tribe.

As a young girl, I lived in tumultuous times for the Jews. Once I shared with my father a vision I received of the Jewish people being captured by an empire from the west. Neither father nor I told anyone else, but he believed I had received foreknowledge from God, for he said, "Anna, you are a prophetess of the Lord. We shall see how Jehovah chooses to use your life."

Over the years, my father told me stories about other prophetesses: Miriam, Deborah, and Huldah. I thought to myself, "Those are famous women, but I am just a poor girl from Kanah."

At fifteen I married Abner. Our seven years together were the happiest years of my life. I was always disappointed that we were not able to have children. But maybe it was just as well, for Abner was killed during the siege when Pompey captured Judea and Syria for the Roman Empire.

After I had grieved for a year, my father asked me to go with him to Jerusalem to get my mind off the past and to encourage me to look to the future. One day soon after our arrival in Jerusalem, my father and I were seated on Solomon's porch overlooking the temple when I received a vision which was to sustain me for the rest of my life. It was a vision of the coming of the Messiah who would redeem Jerusalem.

When I told my father about what I had seen, he said, "Anna, you must remain in the temple area, praying and fasting until the Messiah comes." Of course, there were tears as my father and I parted, but I felt at peace knowing I was doing God's will.

It wasn't long after we had parted that father died. There were days that I missed him so much. Since he was a farmer of the hillsides, I had always found such comfort in walking to the outskirts of the city of Jerusalem to watch the planting. In the fall I would return to the fields to observe the harvest. The cycle of planting and harvest brought such solace to my soul and had come and gone for sixty-two years. My praying and fasting never wavered during that time, even though I had begun to wonder if I would live to see my Messiah.

The season was now winter. Daylight had been lengthening for a month and a half. The crisp air made the sky even bluer. As I finished my morning prayers in the temple, I raised my head to view a beautiful young mother accompanied by her strong husband. The woman was cradling a baby about six weeks old in her arms. As they walked toward my good friend, Simeon, the same voice that had spoken in my vision said, "It is He. The One for whom you have been waiting. You are looking upon the Messiah."

As I watched, Simeon took the child into his arms and said, "Lord, now I can die content, for I have seen the Savior as You promised me I would. He is the light that will shine upon all the nations, and He will be the glory of your people Israel." Next Simeon blessed the baby's mother and father and prophesied of the child's future.

In that instant, I lifted my thanks unto the Lord for I knew I had lived to see the Messiah. From that moment on, I told all who would listen, "This babe is the Messiah, the Savior who will redeem Jerusalem."

Based on Luke 2:22-38; Joshua 19:24-31; Leviticus 12:1-4;
Exodus 15:20; Judges 4:4; II Kings 22:14.

Seraphira: Woman at the Well

My name is Seraphira. I have the worst record for marriage in all of Samaria. Even as a young girl, I was headstrong. My fierce independence grew stronger as a youth when I was told by some young Jews that Samaritans were inferior because they had intermarried with Gentiles. Men are attracted to me because I am pretty, but when they later discover my independent spirit, they hand me a divorce letter. I suppose I am fortunate to have had no children by any of my five husbands. After my fifth divorce, I finally decided to live with a man without the benefit of marriage. Since we aren't married, at least Gershom can't divorce me. Besides he seems to love me.

My home is in Sychar, a Samaritan town thirty miles north of Jerusalem. Most of the women here walk to Jacob's well in the cool of the morning to draw water. I go alone in the heat of midday to avoid the clusters of chatting women. Rather than speaking, they look askance at me because of my reputation. On this late winter day, I began my walk to Jacob's well to fill my pottery jar with water. I had just drawn my jar from the well and set it on the rock wall surrounding the well when a man spoke to me saying, "Give me a drink."

When I turned to face Him, I saw that He was a tall, broad-shouldered man with a handsome face framed with a neatly trimmed, black beard. Noting His Galilean accent, I questioned Him, "How is it that you, a Jew, ask me for a drink since I am a Samaritan and a woman?"

"If you knew the gift of God, and who it is who says to you, 'Give me a drink,' you would have asked Him instead, and He would have given you living water."

When I pointed out to Him that He had no rope or jar to draw the living water, His response was, "Everyone who drinks from this well will thirst again, but whoever drinks my water will thirst no more. The water I give shall become in you a well of water springing up into eternal life."

So I decided to brave it and asked Him to give me some of His water to quench my thirst so I wouldn't have to make so many long walks to the well. But instead of giving me some of His water, He told me to go get my husband and bring him here. When I explained that I had no husband, he said, "Yes, true, but you have been married five times and the man you are living with is not your husband."

Feeling uncomfortable that He knew of my sin and concluding that He must be a prophet, I quickly changed the subject by asking the age old question, "Why do Samaritans worship on this mountain and the Jews in Jerusalem?" But instead of siding with either the Jews or Samaritans, He explained that God is Spirit, and those who worship Him must worship Him in spirit and in truth whether or not they are on the mountain or in Jerusalem.

Since I didn't completely grasp what He was saying, I said, "I know that the Messiah is coming some day, and He will fully explain these things to me."

Then He said to me, "I who speak to you am the Messiah."

Just then a group of men approached from the town calling out His name,

"Jesus!" None asked why He was talking to a Samaritan woman, but I could tell they were perplexed that He would do such a thing.

As for me, I didn't care what they thought. I had just met the Messiah! Quickly I turned to hurry back to the town leaving my waterpot behind. When I finally arrived in the town, I went straight to the gate where the men would gather and boldly adjured them, "Come, see a man who told me all the things that I ever did! Can this be the Messiah?"

Much to my surprise, they listened to me and left the town to see this man of whom I spoke. I decided to stay in the town and tell anyone who would listen. As a result, many in Sychar believed on Him. Those who went out to meet Jesus apparently liked whatever He said because they pleaded with Him to stay with them for a couple of days which He did. Those who heard Him speak told me that they no longer believed just because of what I said, but more so because of what He, Jesus, said.

For days after He left, I could not put Jesus out of my mind. He was the first man I had ever met who didn't put me down. Even when He brought up my lifestyle, I felt that He cared about me. From this day forward, I shall love all the people in Sychar in the same way that Jesus loved me.

Based on John 4:3-42.

Hannah:
The Mother-In-Law

*M*y name is Hannah. I have a large house in Capernaum on the Sea of Galilee. Not long after my husband died, I invited my daughter Judith and her husband Simon to come live with me. I knew my grandchildren would like the move because they have always loved to visit, especially when I make their favorite sweet bread.

Judith and Simon own a small house in Bethsaida, five miles east of Capernaum. With three children and a fourth on the way, things are getting crowded for them. I knew that Simon was close to his father Jonah and his brother Andrew for they had worked together as fishermen since Simon was a boy, so I wasn't sure how he would feel about moving. But to my surprise, he thought a move to Capernaum would be a good thing since Andrew and he had been spending more and more time traveling with Jesus, and Judith was expecting soon.

So the decision to move was made, and it wasn't long until everyone had settled in. What a joy for me to have Judith, Simon, and the children filling up my big house. An added joy was having Andrew so close by as well. He decided to build a small house next to mine so he could be near the children and could easily pick up and travel with Simon whenever Jesus asked them to go.

The children all love having Andrew next door. They crowd into his house whenever he is home to listen to him read them stories about the heroes of the Bible. My grandson likes the stories about David while the girls' favorite is Ruth's marriage to Boaz. I think the children love their uncle so much because they can tell that he genuinely loves them.

Well, things were going along smoothly until one Sabbath morning when I woke up with a fever. I don't remember being sick a day in my life, so you can imagine my concern when I found myself so weak that I didn't even have enough strength to get out of bed.

Simon had gone to the synagogue to hear Jesus expound on the Scriptures, so Judith sent the two eldest children to the well for cool water to dip cloths into to lay across my forehead. I'm not quite sure how much time had passed when I was startled from my rest by Simon's booming voice. He was carrying on about something Jesus had mentioned in His reading when I heard him inviting Jesus, James, John and Andrew to come in for dinner.

Sometimes I think Simon's mouth gets ahead of his brain. What in the world was he thinking? Here I am lying in bed with a fever, and he is out there inviting guests in for dinner. Who does he think is going to feed them? I certainly don't feel up to it. Then before I knew it, I heard the grandchildren saying, "Grandmother is sick in bed, and mother is putting cool cloths on her forehead to make her feel better." Now I was really embarrassed. Not only do I have guests in my house without my knowing they were coming, but now they also know that I'm sick.

Then Simon, whom Jesus calls Peter, came blundering into my room apologizing for inviting guests while I was feeling so bad. His winsome way made it hard for me to hold a grudge against him. I smiled weakly, then he asked if it would be all right if Judith fixed dinner. Of course, I nodded my head "yes" and tried not to let it bother me. When he turned in the doorway to go back down the hall, he almost ran right into Jesus who had been waiting just outside my doorway the whole time. Peter excused himself and went on his way. Then Jesus poked His head around the door frame and asked, "Hannah, may I come in?"

"Oh, yes. I'm so sorry I'm sick, for I know you must be hungry."

Jesus smiled then took my hand and helped me to sit up. At first, I felt a little flushed, but soon the heat which had been radiating off of my body seemed to disappear. When I mentioned to Judith that I felt like the fever had broken, she placed the back of her hand on my forehead. Her relieved expression told me the fever was gone. Much to my delight I was able to get out of bed and pull the curtain back to let the sunshine in.

"Let's see, Judith, what do we have in the pantry that we can fix quickly to feed these men?"

With a twinkle in her eye, Judith grinned at me as she said, "Mother, did you remember to say, 'Thank you?'"

I smiled back, then turned to Jesus and said, "Thank you, Jesus, for healing me."

Jesus acknowledged my appreciation with His warm smile before turning to join the rest of the men in the living room. Judith and I chuckled a little to ourselves then left for the kitchen to fix the hungry men some lunch.

Based on Mark 1:29-34; Luke 4:38-41; Matthew 8:14-15.

Matthew Levi: A Tax Collector

*M*y name is Matthew. My father, Alpheus Levi, and my brothers import many goods for their shop in Jerusalem. A specialty in our family for many generations has been a strong cloth made from long fiber cotton imported from India. Everyone recognizes Levi cotton because of our unique, dark blue dye.

As a young man, I traveled with my father and brothers to Caesarea Maritima, the major port for Judea, to restock our inventory. A Roman official in this grand city, who was aware of the business skills of my family, asked me to be a tax collector for the Roman government. He offered to assign me to the Capernaum area so I wouldn't have to collect from friends and relatives. The tax collectors were allowed to keep five percent as a motivation to insure that no tax went uncollected. However, some publicans were known to demand more than what was due and keep that for themselves as well.

I accepted the job and moved to Capernaum beside the Sea of Galilee. The taxes were easy to collect because of the presence of a Roman army century. However, when I took the job, I hadn't thought about it limiting my circle of friends. As it turned out, the only people who would associate with me were the publicans, for the Jews hated me for taking their hard-earned money and giving it to Rome.

As a boy, I had attended school in the synagogue, where I learned about the history of my people from the Pentateuch and the prophets. Isaiah told of a time coming when the Romans would no longer tax the Jews because the Jewish Messiah would come to rule our part of the world.

Then one Sabbath I was in the synagogue listening to the reading of the scrolls when a new teacher from Nazareth read from Isaiah. I was convinced that His claim of being the Messiah was true. So when He came by my office and said, "Follow Me," I walked away from my good-paying job to become his disciple.

That day I invited all of my friends to a party at my house so they could meet this teacher and His other disciples. When the Pharisees saw Jesus headed toward my house, they asked His disciples, "Why does Jesus eat with tax collectors and sinners?"

When Jesus heard the question, He replied, "Those who are well have no need of a physician, but those who are sick do. As for you, I desire mercy on your part rather than sacrifices."

Jesus always spoke in parables. Sometimes He explained the meaning, and sometimes He didn't. He turned to my friends and said, "No one puts new wine into old wineskins, for the new wine will burst the old skins, ruining the skins and spilling the wine."

I didn't understand this saying at first, but it kept replaying itself in my mind. Eventually I came to believe that He meant that His new teachings of grace cannot be contained within the old forms of the law. This saying was only one of the many which He shared with us. I attempted to keep a record of them in my daily log but oftentimes became so busy with the day's affairs that I could only write down a phrase or so to jog my memory later on.

Eventually Jesus chose me to be one of His apostles. I'm not sure why He chose me, but I believe there must have been a very good reason. I thought I understood why He chose Judas. He seemed like the kind of man you could trust. Jesus even let him handle all of the money! But do you know that he was the very one who turned traitor and betrayed Him with a kiss?

My mother kept telling me to write all of this down, but I couldn't see the benefit of a written copy of Jesus' story which might be passed around among a few Jews for awhile then would be lost.

My mother always said, "Of all the Levis, you are the most hardheaded." Now after about twenty years, I have decided to listen to my mother and write down Jesus' story, and I am calling it, "The Gospel According to Matthew."

Based on Matthew 9:9-17; Mark 2:14-22; Luke 5:27-38; John 1:17.

Claudius: The Roman Centurion with Great Faith

*M*y name is Claudius. As a boy my family lived in Rome where my father served as an officer in the army. My father insisted I study mathematics and Greek and Hebrew, in addition to Latin.

At the age of sixteen I joined the Roman Legion and was sent to serve in Africa. After my tour in Africa was completed, I was promoted to sergeant before being assigned to a post in Spain. I married Aprilia, the little neighbor girl who used to send me love notes through my cousin, and took her with me to Spain. At first my parents resisted the idea of a love marriage as opposed to an arranged marriage, but eventually they gave in as they agreed with my choice and loved Aprilia nearly as much as I. We were hardly married a year before our first son arrived. The next two boys were born after we were transferred to Gaul.

Aprilia was always a wonderful wife and mother. During the early years of our marriage, I was required to be away weeks at a time with the legion on peacekeeping missions. Aprilia, with the help of tutors, schooled the boys in the same subjects I had studied at their age. Aprilia adjusted to the ways of whatever country we were in and always seemed happy. Even though she said nothing, I sensed that she wished she had had a daughter.

General Tiberius, who was to become Caesar, promoted me to centurion and assigned me to the command of the century stationed in Capernaum, Galilee. Not long after our arrival, Aprilia began a search for household help. Ketura, a young teenager, came looking for work as an indentured servant. She would be given a thousand leptons which she could then give to her poor family when she agreed to work for Aprilia for three years. The agreement could be continued after that, if Ketura so wished. Ketura was happy because the food and housing were better than that at home, so after her three years of servitude, Ketura agreed to work for another three.

As the years passed by, I could see that Aprilia had grown very fond of Ketura. Part of this fondness could have been elicited by Ketura's excellent work, but I wondered if the feeling was also that of a mother for the daughter Aprilia never had.

Even I began to respect the Galileans more than I had ever expected. They were a devout people and made my peacekeeping job easier because they strove to live by the ten commandments which were given to them by Yahweh through their leader Moses nearly 1500 years ago.

It has now been ten years since I took command of the hundred men in my century. Five years ago the Jews were attempting to rebuild their rather decrepit synagogue with whatever materials they could acquire. Most of the Roman tax was sent to Rome, but a portion was left with me for spending at my discretion. Because I had grown to care about the Jewish people and respected their devotion to their God, I chose to buy the material for the new synagogue.

The Jewish elders seemed genuinely grateful.

Since I am a Gentile, a Jew will not enter my house, for if he does, he believes he will be defiled. I was free, however, to enter their synagogue and listen to those speaking. By listening, I was better able to understand the ways of the people I had been sent to govern.

A few months ago a Jew named Jesus moved to Capernaum from Nazareth. He spoke in the synagogue about God with an authority that no other speaker I had heard possessed. I had received reports from reliable sources that this Jesus had the power to heal the sick.

Then one spring morning I was awakened early by Aprilia who said, "I have been up all night with Ketura. Her illness has worsened, and I fear she is at the point of death"

I knew the seriousness of Ketura's condition when I saw tears in Aprilia's eyes and heard her voice break as she explained to me the situation. I also knew how important Ketura was to Aprilia and how Ketura had grown to become more of a daughter than a servant.

Remembering the reports of Jesus' healings, I called on the elders of the synagogue, asking them to go find Jesus so He could bring healing to Ketura. These good friends left immediately to find Jesus.

Not long after they left, I realized I was asking Jesus, a Jew, to enter a Gentile's home. Right away I sent other friends to tell Jesus He would not have to come but that all He needed to do was to speak a word from where He was, and my servant would be healed.

I told Aprilia about the request I had sent to Jesus, then I walked outside and down the path to the gate to receive the report from my friends. I hadn't been down there long when I saw Aprilia's profile appear in the doorway. She stepped out onto the porch and began to run down the long path. As she drew nearer, I could see a broad smile on her face. Then she threw her arms around me saying, "Ketura has had a sudden improvement. The fever has left her and she is alert and bright-eyed."

After giving Aprilia a warm squeeze, I released her and turned to open the gate for my friends who were now approaching. The leader of the group stood before me and began quoting Jesus: "I am amazed. Among all the Jews in Israel, I have not met one with such a faith as Claudius who believed I could heal from a distance. Tell him that his faith has healed Ketura."

Based on Luke 7:1-10; Matthew 8:5-13.

Ariella: A Woman from Nain

My name is Ariella. I live in Nain, Galilee, which is six miles south of Nazareth, with my son Galen. When my husband Hector and I were first married, I joined him in his store where we sold staples and vegetables to those living in Nain and the surrounding countryside. Since our home is attached to the back of our store, it seemed natural for Galen to help with the business as a young boy.

Though I had asked Jehovah for many years for a daughter, this was not His will. Nevertheless the three of us were a very happy family. Hector was firm yet fair in running the store. In spite of Hector's firmness in business matters, he always treated me gently. As a boy, Galen enjoyed playing with the children in our village, but he was always ready to come inside when I called, for he liked to learn about the scales and counting money just as much as he liked to play.

Galen learned much at the school in our synagogue, but he learned even more from his father. When customers were not in the store, I would pretend to be lost in my weaving. My heart would be warmed as I listened to Hector explaining to Galen about fair markup for each item in the store. The markup for staples like barley, raisins, figs, salt, and spices was set. Vegetable prices varied based upon the spoilage of the various produce items. Of course, people always liked to bargain, so we had a secret price range with a fixed minimum.

A year ago, however, my happiness was shattered when Hector complained of a terrible pain in his chest, then collapsed in the aisle of the store. I felt so helpless. There was nothing I could do but pray and tell my neighbor to quickly find a physician. When he arrived, he said that Hector died just moments after he had experienced the pain. Galen, now a responsible sixteen-year-old, stepped in to manage the store just as his father had run it. He was a great comfort to me during my months of grieving.

I had just begun to accept my circumstances when my life was shattered once more. Galen was returning from Maritina Caesarea with supplies for the store when he was ambushed by robbers and killed.

So I had no alternative but to prepare for my second funeral in the space of a year. There were times that I felt so numb and empty inside, but many women from the village who had been our customers stood beside me. No one knew exactly what to say, but I found their presence comforting. On the day of the funeral, the men left their workplaces to be there as well. As the funeral procession moved from the synagogue through the city gate on the way to the burial site, my heart was so broken that I was unable to control my weeping. Two of my husband's friends physically supported me as I retraced the steps taken during his funeral one year ago.

As the procession made its way through the gate, a tall man followed by a crowd of people approached me. At first I was a little apprehensive because I had never seen Him before and didn't know what it was that He wanted. But when He spoke and said in a soothing, compassionate voice, "Do not weep," my fears seemed to fade away.

I felt such a peace come over me that I stopped crying and watched this stranger as He walked over to my son's coffin and laid His hands on it. The pallbearers appeared stunned and didn't know exactly what to do, so they stood still.

Then in a strong, clear voice this stranger said, "Young man, I say to you, arise!"

My heart leaped with expectation at His words. Then without any further warning Galen sat up. When he saw the man standing by his coffin, it was almost as if he knew Him, and he reached up to Him. The man helped Galen out of the coffin and brought him to me. With tears streaming down my face, I embraced my son for he had been dead and was now alive.

With great amazement the townspeople began to praise Jehovah and say, "A great prophet has appeared among us. Jehovah has visited His people to care for them."

Now I knew who He was. He was a prophet. I had never met a prophet before, so I asked Him, "Who are you?"

Then in a calm voice He replied, "My name is Jesus."

"You must be the prophet from Nazareth who the people say is the Son of God." When I reached out to thank Him, His large hands engulfed mine, and I asked, "How can I ever thank you Jesus?"

"Ariella, all that I ask is that you continue to love all My children in Nain as you have in the past, for as you love them, you are also loving Me."

Based on Luke 7:11-17.

Jairus:
The Return of a Daughter

*M*y name is Jairus and I live in Capernaum on the west side of the Sea of Galilee. The Lord has blessed me with a prosperous fish-drying business. I work closely with Zebedee and Jonah and their sons—James, John, Simon, and Andrew, who are commercial fisherman. An even more significant blessing was the Lord's gift of a daughter later in life. Most would have given up hope by middle age, but not my wife Leah. She kept telling me about Sarah. Eventually she did give birth to a girl whom we named Abby, which means source of joy.

Twelve years have passed since Abby's birth, and I have tried to be a good father and at the same time a good citizen. Several years ago the rabbi took me aside and asked me to serve as ruler of our synagogue. My responsibilities would be supervising the worship service, running the weekly school, and caring for the buildings. The workers at my fish-drying business were loyal and honest, so I was able to divide my time between my business and the synagogue. I enjoyed this new responsibility because I could be around the students in the school.

For many months a man named Jesus, who had moved to Capernaum from Nazareth, had been a regular speaker in our synagogue. I loved to listen to Jesus because He knew the Scriptures so well. Sometimes He would tell a parable to make a point more understandable. But while I enjoyed Jesus, I knew the Pharisees didn't, for they were often the object of Jesus' criticism.

Recently, Abby awoke in the night with a high fever. Over the next few days, Leah and I and the doctor did everything we could to make her well, but the illness only worsened. Abby even lost interest in the new lamb she had been caring for.

In times past, when Andrew delivered fish, he had told me stories about Jesus healing the sick. Up until now I had not talked to Jesus because I feared that the Pharisees would ask me to resign from my job as ruler.

But in my desperation, I decided to take the risk and began to look for Jesus. Upon finding Him, I fell at His feet and begged Him saying, "My little daughter is at the point of death. Please come and lay your hands on her, that she may get well and live."

I don't know whether it was because of my desperation or because of my daughter's illness that He came, but He said not another word and went along with me. When we rounded the last corner on the road to my house, Thad, my messenger, appeared walking swiftly toward us. I knew he had bad news for me because of the expression on his face. Thad could hardly speak, but he finally managed to blurt out, "Abby is dead, so there is no use in troubling Jesus now."

Dead? She couldn't be. She is my little girl. I turned to look up into the eyes of Jesus, and He looked back at me with a steady gaze and said, "Don't be afraid, Jairus, only believe."

As we approached my house, we could hear the people inside loudly weeping and wailing. But this didn't seem to stop Jesus as He walked into their midst and said, "Why all this weeping and wailing? The child isn't dead. She is only asleep!"

Of course, the people laughed and jeered at Him saying, "Don't you think we recognize a dead person when we see one?"

Then Jesus told them all to leave. Everyone suddenly became very quiet and one by one got up from their place on the floor mat and walked out of the house. Then He motioned for Leah and me along with Simon, James, and John to come with Him into Abby's room. Her lifeless little body lay limply on the bed covered by the blanket her grandmother had woven for her birthday.

Then Jesus walked up beside the bed and took Abby's hand in His saying, "Get up, little girl!"

Immediately Abby's big brown eyes opened, she pushed back the covers, sat up, and looked around. Still holding Jesus' hand, she let Him help her to her feet. With a smile Abby held out her arms to her mother who reached to embrace her. Leah's cheeks were wet with tears of joy as she hugged her little girl. After a few moments, Abby looked at me over her mother's shoulder and asked about her lamb.

Unable to contain myself any longer, I grabbed Abby from her mother's arms and swung her round and round. With tears unashamedly rolling down my cheeks, I turned to Jesus and said, "Thank you. You have brought me life."

Then Jesus said a very peculiar thing. He told me not to tell anyone and to get Abby something to eat. Getting her a fruit to eat was no problem, but how could I keep the rest of this a secret?

Based on Mark 5:22-24,35-42; Luke 8:41-42,49-56; Matt. 4:21,16:17.

Jobina: An Unclean Woman

*M*y name is Jobina. My home is in Capernaum. I have a physical infirmity that began twelve years ago when I was twelve years old. It was then that I first began to have a continual slow discharge of blood. The doctor told my mother and father that I would outgrow my problem. The months grew into years, and still the problem did not go away.

By my sixteenth birthday, most of the other girls my age had been promised in marriage by their fathers. But my father could not offer me in marriage because he knew I remained unclean. As this reality began to sink in, I began to wish that I could just die. Eventually, however, I accepted the fact that I would never marry and have children.

From the time I was a small girl, my mother had taught me how to weave cloth from the wool of our sheep, so I began my own business in woolen materials. In a very short time, I became wealthy as people sought out my quality workmanship. Inside me, there was still a flicker of hope that the doctors would come up with a new discovery and that I would be able to marry and have children. So I spent all of my wealth on doctors in an attempt to find a cure for my uncontrolled bleeding. I even traveled to other cities across Galilee, Samaria, and Judea seeking help. With each new doctor, my hope grew. But eventually they too would tell me that there was nothing they could do, and I would plummet into deep depression.

One morning when I was returning from the synagogue, a trusted friend of mine told me that her friend, Hannah, had been sick with a fever and was healed by a man named Jesus. If He could heal Hannah, I reasoned, then He could heal me. My hope began to soar and immediately I knew what I must do. I would search out Jesus for my healing.

My friend had said that Jesus was scheduled to speak this coming Sabbath in the synagogue and should be arriving any day now. Three days came and went, then one morning, when I was busy weaving wool, an older boy passed along my street telling everyone that Jesus' boat had come in from the other side of the Sea of Galilee. Immediately I put down the cloth I was weaving and rushed to join the crowd that was quickly forming and following after the boy.

When we finally found Jesus, people were pressing in on Him from all sides. Some came out of curiosity, but many were there seeking healing. Because of the size of the crowd, I didn't see how I could possibly talk with Jesus. "If only I can touch Him," I thought, "I will be healed." I held my head cover across my face so the townspeople would not know an unclean woman was amongst them. I leaned over and pushed my way toward Jesus. Though buffeted by the crowd I pressed on until I reached Him. I then fell to my knees, and reaching out my clutching fingers found the hem of His garment. Immediately a warmth flooded all of my insides, and in that moment, I knew I was cured. Then I released my hold as quickly as I had grasped it.

Just then Jesus stopped abruptly, looked around at the crowd, and asked, "Who touched me?"

Haltingly, I began to stand, but I kept silent. I was a bit relieved when a large man in the crowd spoke up and said, "Master, the multitudes surround you and press you on every side."

But Jesus shook His head and said, "It was more than a touch. I felt the healing power go out from me."

It was then that I pulled away my head covering and saw Jesus clearly for the first time. He was taller than those who gathered around Him, and His weathered face shone with a gentle smile. With this my courage returned, and I spoke up and said, "Lord, it was I."

Then with kind eyes He turned to me and said, "Daughter, your faith has made you well. Go in peace and be freed from your suffering."

Based on Mark 5:25-34; Matthew 9:20-22; Luke 8:43-48.

Cora, the Syrophoenician: A Desperate Mother

I am a Greek, a Syrophoenician by birth, who had recently come northwest from Canaan to live in the region of Tyre and Sidon. As a single mother, I was filled with terror when my only child, Angela, who had just turned five, was suddenly attacked by a demon. The demon convulsed Angela throwing her to the floor.

Angela and her only toy, a stuffed sheepskin doll, are inseparable. When I get busy with housework, I often hear Angela carrying on a conversation with her doll. I knew Angela was extremely ill when she cast her doll aside. I was in a quandary as to what I should do since I had no money for a doctor.

As I walked to the well to draw water to cool Angela, a young man from the village came by and announced that Jesus had entered a house nearby. I had heard stories about this man named Jesus who could heal people by driving out their demons. But He is a Jew, and I am a Gentile, and Jews and Gentiles aren't the best of friends. Still I thought, "He must listen to me for Angela's sake." I was determined to seek Him out to ask Him to heal my daughter.

Dropping my bucket, I ran to look for Jesus. When I found the house, people were crowded around the open doorway so I slipped in. My eyes rested on the One speaking who appeared to be the leader. He was a powerfully built man—tall and with broad shoulders. From where I stood, I could feel love emanating from Him and concluded that this must be the man named Jesus. But would He, a Jew, listen to me, a Gentile who is just a woman? For my daughter's sake, He must.

Without another thought, I began to push my way through the crowded room. When I got close enough to touch Him, I threw myself at His feet and cried out, "Have mercy on me, O Lord, Son of David; my daughter, Angela, is severely possessed by a demon."

But Jesus did not answer even a word. Then one of the men with Him pointed to the door and said, "Send her away."

Jesus went on as though the order hadn't been given and responded by saying, "I was sent only to the lost sheep of the house of Israel."

His friendly eyes and kind face belied His unkind words, so I knelt before Him and said, "Lord help me."

Jesus answered, "It is not fair to take the children's bread and throw it to the dogs."

This Jew's words to me, a Gentile, were harsh, but His demeanor was compassionate, so I said, "Yes, Lord, yet even the dogs eat the crumbs that fall from their master's table."

Then Jesus smiled and said, "Cora, great is your faith. Go your way for your daughter, Angela, is healed."

Somewhat surprised, I got off of my knees and gathered the cloth of my garment in my hand so I could stand. But before I turned to rush home, I touched Jesus on the arm and said, "Thank you!"

When I reached my house, I threw open the door to find Angela cuddling and talking to her doll. I was so relieved to see Angela at play and well again. It was then that I realized that the harsh words He had spoken were to test my faith.

Based on Mark 7:24-30 and Matthew 15:21-28.

Zebedee:
The Well-Known Fisherman

My name is Zebedee. My ancestors have been well-known as fishermen for many generations. I would say that Jonah is the only other fisherman as good as I. Jonah and I began fishing together as young boys with our fathers. Jonah and I work closely with our friend Jairus who has a fish-drying business in Capernaum only five miles east of where we live in Bethsaida. Together, we meet the needs of the people in our surrounding area for nourishing fish year round.

Jehovah has blessed me with a good wife, Salome, and two fine sons, James and John. Jonah has been similarly blessed, and he has two sons named Simon and Andrew. In my generation, fathers taught their sons how to work hard at their profession. Jonah and I have spent many hours giving the boys painstaking instructions on ways to find the fish and how to handle the net to capture the most fish. Because of this, our sons have become good fishermen. With the exception of Jonah and me, they are the best on the Sea of Galilee.

I, as most fathers, planned for my boys to carry on the family business. I suppose each of us wants our name to carry on after we are gone. Everyone remembers my father and my grandfather because of their successful fishing business, and now they remember me because I have continued to build on their business.

Until very recently things were going wonderfully well. James and John were fishing with me, and Simon and Andrew had joined Jonah in his business.

Then one day, out of the blue, an itinerant preacher named Jesus came along and made some lofty promise to my sons about making them fishers of men, and they believed him. So they just up and left their boats to follow this preacher.

This younger generation just doesn't get it. They don't understand the value of a tradition such as a family business. If the boys don't come to their senses soon and get back to work fishing, future generations will not even remember who they are, and what a shame that would be!

Based on Mark 1:16-20; Matthew 16:17.

Uriah: I Believe —
Help My Unbelief

*M*y name is Uriah. My home is in Nain, six miles southeast of Nazareth. My son Ben, who recently turned twelve, has been possessed by a demon since he was a small child. Whenever it seizes him, it dashes him down and he foams at the mouth, grinds his teeth, and becomes rigid from head to toe. I have prayed to Jehovah for years for Ben's deliverance, but He has not seemed to hear me.

Almost every day the boys in the neighborhood gather for a game of throwing around a sheepskin ball that has been stuffed tightly with wool and sewn shut. The other boys have shunned Ben because his seizures frighten them. This has been especially painful for Ben and for me because, other than the seizures, he is just like any other boy.

When I heard that Jesus was in the nearby countryside, I knew I needed to find Him and ask Him to heal Ben, for stories were widespread that He had healed other children. Taking Ben with me, I followed those on the road to the foot of Mount Tabor where we found a crowd surrounding nine of Jesus' disciples. Holding Ben's hand tightly, I pressed my way through the crowd so that I could talk to the disciples. I asked them to heal Ben, but none were able.

About that time I could see four men coming down from Mount Tabor. Still holding tightly to Ben's hand, I hurried to stay at the front of the crowd which was swarming towards the four. I explained to the people why I needed to ask Jesus to heal Ben. Others argued with me saying that their need for healing was equally as urgent.

The one in the front of those approaching from the mountain, a tall, broad-shouldered man, appeared to be the leader. When He reached those of us at the front of the crowd, He asked, "What's all the argument about?"

I stepped forward to say, "I have brought my son for you to heal of a dumb spirit. I begged your disciples to cast out the demon, but they couldn't do it."

Jesus looked directly at His disciples and said, "Oh, what tiny faith you have; how much longer must I be with you? Bring the boy to me."

Jesus knelt down so His face was at the same level as Ben's. His eyes were friendly, and His expression was kind.

Then, as if the demon was to have the last say, it convulsed Ben and threw him to the ground. As was normally the case with Ben's demonic attacks, the crowd shrank back in horror.

Jesus' eyes met mine as He asked, "How long has he been this way?"

"Since he was very small. Sometimes the demon makes him fall into the fire or into the water. Oh, have mercy on us and do something if you can."

"If I can? Anything is possible if you only have faith."

"I do have faith; oh, help me to have more faith!"

Jesus turned back to Ben saying, "O demon of deafness and dumbness, I command you to come out of Ben and enter him no more!"

The demon convulsed Ben one more time then left him lying limp on the ground.

Whispers in the crowd could be heard saying, "He is dead."

Jesus' eyes stayed fixed on Ben. His face radiated compassion. Then Jesus took Ben gently by the hand and helped him to his feet. Ben looked over at me as if to get approval then shyly hugged this One who had delivered him from his torment. Jesus smiled as He reached down and tousled Ben's hair with His large hand.

The only one experiencing more joy than I, was Ben. With his young face framed by a wide smile, he said, "Now I can play ball like all the other boys." It was then that I knew that Ben would never be troubled by demons again.

Based on Mark 9:14-27; Matthew 17:14-18.

Dara: The Little Girl Who Drew Near To Jesus

*M*y name is Dara. I am eight years old and I have a younger brother, Seth, who is five. Sometimes I see my friend, Yoby, who lives in a two room house in Jericho. One time when we were playing dolls, she turned to me and said, "I feel sorry for you because you live in such a tiny house. You must be poor."

I had never thought about being poor but decided that Yoby was probably right. I felt sorry for Yoby because she had no brothers or sisters, and I had Seth to play with. Sometimes Mother would take Seth and me down to the edge of the Jordan River to play. I would build a sand house with two rooms like Yoby's and imagine that Seth and I had lots of room to play.

Today my mother took Seth and me with her to a hillside near the river to listen to a teacher named Jesus. The crowd was still gathering when Mother took Seth and me by the hand to try to get closer to Jesus. Other mothers were trying to get closer with their children too.

When we were just a short distance from Jesus, Mother, still holding our hands, kneeled down between Seth and me. Then she placed Seth's hand in mine and said, "Dara, I want you to take Seth with you and walk up beside Jesus. People have told me He will bless you, and things will be better."

I was scared, but I squeezed Seth's hand tightly and pretended to be brave so that Seth wouldn't be afraid. As I pulled Seth along through a group of men, all I could see were sandals and robes of blue, green, red, and purple. Then one man yelled out, "Go on! Get out of here! This is no place for children!"

Now I was really scared! When Seth could see that I was frightened, he began to cry. One of the men on the edge of the group knelt down and took both Seth's and my hand. He said, "My name is Andrew. Don't be afraid. Judas, the one yelling at you, doesn't understand about children."

Still holding our hands, Andrew led us to a nearby rock and said, "Here, you sit awhile with me so you can see Jesus."

Seth's gaze was fixed on Andrew. His crying stopped, and he began to smile because Andrew was smiling at him.

I turned to watch Jesus. He was bigger than the other men. I kept looking at His eyes, for they sparkled in a way that made me know that He must love Seth and me. In a little while, He raised His arms and reached out toward the children and their mothers saying, "Let the little children come to me, for the kingdom of God belongs to such as they."

The kingdom part I didn't understand, but I knew that Jesus wanted me to come to Him. So I pulled Seth by the hand and walked right up beside Jesus where He was sitting on a big rock. When I leaned against His leg, He picked up Seth and sat him on His lap. He put one hand on Seth's head and His other one on me. I glanced at Seth. He was smiling. Then I looked up at Jesus as He said, "Bless you and thank you for bringing your brother so I could bless him too."

"Since we have been blessed, will we no longer be poor?"

"Now you will be rich in love, and someday you will understand that this is more important than a two room house."

I turned to hurry back to Mother to share the good news. As we drew near she knelt down to greet us. When I told her that Jesus said, "We are going to be rich in love," she began to cry. Seth looked bewildered, for Mother never cried. Soon he was crying too.

"Mother, why are you crying? Are you sad?"

As her strong arms gathered Seth and me to her breast, she said, "No, dear, I am overcome with happiness." Then Mother placed Seth's hand in hers and held my hand tightly with her other as we began our journey back to our tiny home so full of love.

Based on Mark 10:13-16.

Amiel: A Rich Young Ruler

*M*y name is Amiel. My home is in the town of Julias in the district of Peraea. Peraea lies along the eastern side of the Jordan River, just north of the Dead Sea. I am known as the ruler of Julias because my family owns most of the property in this village. My father and grandfather oversee more extensive holdings all across Peraea. When I reached the age of sixteen, my grandfather put me in charge of the village of Julias so I could learn to manage property.

Some travelers passing through my village told me about a Galilean named Jesus. They said He was teaching about Jehovah and heaven when they went through Jericho. I decided to go to Jericho to look for this teacher to see if He could answer my questions about heaven. When I found Him, I joined a group of Pharisees who were questioning Jesus about divorce and the coming of the Kingdom of God. As they finished, I asked my question, "Good Teacher, what must I do to enter heaven?"

Jesus said, "Why do you call me good? No one is good except God alone. You know the commandments: 'Do not murder. Do not commit adultery. Do not steal. Do not bear false witness. Do not defraud. Honor your father and mother.'"

I felt relieved and assured of a place in heaven since I had observed all these things since my youth. As I looked into Jesus' compassionate eyes, I felt His love for me. I was unprepared, however, for the next words spoken: "One thing you lack; go, and sell all you possess, and give to the poor, and you shall have treasure in heaven; and come, follow me."

My shoulders drooped and my face fell in sadness, for I owned much property. A little embarrassed, I moved away from the crowd and the group of Pharisees who had been questioning Jesus. I could not bring myself to look at Jesus, but I could clearly hear His voice as He talked to His men: "How hard it will be for those who are wealthy to enter the kingdom of God. It is easier for a camel to go through the eye of a needle than for a rich man to enter the kingdom of God."

Just as I was beginning to be overcome by complete hopelessness, I heard Jesus say to His disciples, "With men it is impossible, but not with God; for all things are possible with God."

Were these words said to offer me some hope? Wanting to think over what He had said, I found a large rock and sat down. After awhile, one of Jesus' men sat down beside me, but I didn't look up. In the background Jesus continued to instruct His disciples about giving and receiving. The one who had joined me laid his hand on my shoulder and said, "My name is Andrew. I have been traveling with Jesus and listening to Him teach across Galilee and now Judea."

I turned to Andrew and asked, "What must I do? I thought my riches were a sign that I was in God's favor."

"No, Amiel, eternal life is equally available for the poor and the rich. Both must be good stewards of whatever they have. But more importantly you must give God first place in your life, not your material wealth. If this means giving everything to the poor, then that's what you must do."

"Now I see why Jesus says it is hard."

"The twelve apostles have left a house or brothers or sisters or mother or father or children or farms for Jesus' sake. Jesus said, 'For this you shall receive rewards both here and in heaven where many who are first will be last, and where the last will be first.'"

"Andrew, I admire you for what you have given up for Jesus. I hope I will have the courage to do the same."

Based on Mark 10:17-31; Matthew 19:16-30; Luke 18:18-30.

Bartimaeus: I Once Was Blind, but Now I See

$\mathcal{M}$y name is Bartimaeus. The people in my home town of Jericho call me the blind beggar, but it was not always this way.

As a boy, I attended school at the synagogue. My favorite reading was the scroll of the prophet Isaiah, who lived seven hundred years ago. Isaiah told of a Messiah who would come to save the Jewish people. My father, Timaeus, owns a shop where he sells tools for tilling the soil. While growing up, my job was to arrange the stock of spades, hoes, picks, pitchforks, scythes, and rakes. As an older boy, I traveled with my father to the port of Caesarea Maritima, which lies sixty miles northwest of Jerusalem. Here ships would dock from all parts of the Roman Empire. The traders would sell us tools to stock our shop.

Carmen had been my special friend since we both turned twelve. In our seventeenth year we were married in our local synagogue. I worked in my father's shop while Carmen stayed busy at home. Two years later, when Carmen discovered she was pregnant, no one could have been more excited than I. I felt a warm anticipation as I imagined caring for Carmen and our baby.

During the week that followed, I had to trust Carmen's care to her mother while I made a spring trip to Caesarea Maritima with my father. I had already handled some merchandise from an African ship before I noticed that several

68

of the crew had eyes swollen shut with infection. On the journey home, my eyes began to burn, so my father and I spent the night in Jerusalem. Before leaving for Jericho, my father sought out a doctor to look at my eyes. After examining me, the doctor said, "This disease will leave you blind. Once the infection clears up, you can safely be with your family."

I was devastated. Would I not see my baby? Must I become a beggar as was the custom in my land for the blind? Jehovah, why me?

My father asked me to continue to sell tools at the shop, but I didn't want to be a burden to the business, so I decided that I should beg for a living. Carmen respected whatever decision I felt would be the best for all involved and agreed to help me to a certain street in the city where I could beg. You can't imagine how embarrassed I felt, yet I had to get money for my family somehow.

Six months passed and Carmen gave birth to a baby girl whom we named Tamara. The first time I picked her up I could feel the whisper of her breath upon my cheek. I couldn't help but squeeze her close to me. The heart in her soft little body beat gently against my chest as I kissed her tiny neck and smelled the sweet smell of a baby. As I cradled her in my arms and sang her a lullaby, I asked Jehovah, "Is it fair that I can't see my baby?" But when I finished the lullaby, there was only silence.

Both of our mothers helped with the care of the baby until Carmen was strong again. And with each day that passed I fervently begged for money so that I could provide for the increased needs of Tamara and Carmen.

The fall harvest had come and gone twice since Tamara was born, and the spring planting season would soon be underway. My begging kept food on the table for Tamara and Carmen, and for this I was grateful. A big help had come from the advice of another beggar, Caleb, who had been blind from birth. He suggested that I wear a decrepit coat to increase the sympathy of my donors, so I decided to take his advice.

Then one day Caleb told me about a man named Jesus who had spoken to the crowds in Jericho. Caleb had heard that Jesus, a descendant of David, had healed a blind man. I caught my breath as I remembered with hope the words of Isaiah about the Messiah: "To open blind eyes . . . And I will lead the blind by a way they do not know, in paths they do not know I will guide them. I will make darkness into light before them . . . ".

Before I was blind, I assumed the blindness spoken of was a figurative blindness, a spiritual one. But now I dared to hope the Scriptures could be referring to my physical ailment as well.

Then one morning when I met Caleb to beg he said, "Let's go to the road that leads to Bethany. Jesus passed this way going east this morning, and they say He is to return through Jericho on the way to His friend's house in Bethany."

So I followed Caleb to the road. As the day rolled along, I could tell by the feel of the sun on my face that the time had reached afternoon. The hubbub of the crowd began softly then quickened, so I asked of anyone who might answer, "Is Jesus coming?"

A nearby woman said in a breathless voice, "Yes, it is He."

So I began to shout, "Jesus, Son of David, have mercy on me!"

A man yelled back at me, "Shut up, you blind beggar!"

But I cried out even louder as I thought about taking care of Tamara and Carmen. Then I heard a commanding voice say, "Tell him to come here."

Those around me nudged me forward saying, "Jesus is calling for you. Jesus is calling for you."

When it finally sunk in that He was calling for me, I yanked off my old coat and threw it aside then jumped up and moved in the direction of the voice I had heard. Then He spoke again with the same authority, "What do you want me to do for you?"

I answered, "Master, let me have my sight back so I can see my daughter Tamara."

Then Jesus said, "Go your way. Your faith has made you whole."

And immediately I received my sight and followed Jesus on the way.

Based on Mark 10:46-52; Matthew 20:29-34; Isaiah 42:6-7,16.

Zacchaeus: A Problem with Self-Esteem

*M*y home is in Jericho, a town fifteen miles northeast of Jerusalem. My people first arrived in Jericho fourteen hundred years ago when Joshua fought a famous battle here. You might think I would be proud and happy to be a citizen of this great city. Not so, I have never been happy.

As a boy I had dreamed of being a great leader like Joshua but my dreams were dashed when I began attending school at the synagogue. Recess was always the same. The two boys who were the leaders would choose sides to play keep-away with a wool yarn ball. Every time, I was chosen last, for you see I am very short.

Eventually my father and my brothers became successful traders. When sellers intimidated me, my brothers told me I was not needed in the business and that I should find other work.

Their continual rejection of me left me sad, but I was still determined to show everyone that I was as good as they were. My opportunity came when the Roman rulers asked me to be the superintendent of customs for the district of Jericho. My friends and family considered me a traitor, but I was determined to show them up by becoming rich.

To increase my riches, I began to collect more than the Romans required, keeping the extra for myself. I just knew that when I became rich enough I would be happy. But the more I had the more I wanted, and instead of becoming happy I grew increasingly more sad.

The wise man, Jesus, who had been teaching in the synagogues and on the hillsides was coming into Jericho. He would know what I should do to find happiness. I was determined to see Him because I just knew He could solve my problem. After a lifetime of reminders, I did not need another to know that I would not be able to see Jesus over the crowd unless I climbed the sycamore tree beside the road. And that is what I decided to do.

I had just found a comfortable seat on a large branch when I heard some commotion down below. It was Jesus. He was a big broad-shouldered man with a friendly face. When He heard the rustling of the branches, He looked up. Then in a loud voice He said, "Zacchaeus! You come down! For I'm going to your house today!"

Hurriedly I climbed down the tree. Jesus was waiting for me. It had been a long time since anyone had been over to my house. I invited some of the people who were traveling with Jesus to come as well. I felt a certain satisfaction in having my living room filled with laughter. Everyone seemed to be enjoying themselves so much that I began to wonder if maybe I had missed the reason for having all the money anyway.

When the laughter died down, I cleared my throat then stood to my feet. In a gesture of friendship, I raised my cup to make a toast, "From now on I will give half of my wealth to the poor, and if I find I have overcharged anyone on his taxes, I will penalize myself by giving back four times as much!"

At first the room was quiet then, one by one, everyone joined in the toast saying a hearty, "Amen!" I wasn't quite sure, however, what Jesus was thinking. But in a moment, He rose to His feet and a hush came over the crowd. Then, all at once, He threw up His arms and said, "Truly, salvation has come to this house today."

Based on Luke 19:1-10.

Mary Magdalene: In His Service

*M*y home is in Magdala on the west side of the Sea of Galilee. I am a cobbler, as was my father before me. My daughter, Mary Magdalene who is sixteen, works with me in the business. The customers all love Mary because she is genuinely interested in them. The fact that she looks like her mother only endears her to them more.

Her mother, Rebecca, and I were sweethearts when we were young. Our friendship waned during the years that boys had nothing to do with girls. But as we grew older, our love was renewed, and eventually we were married. I was glad our friendship had begun early in our lives; otherwise, I might not have won Rebecca, for she was the most beautiful girl in all the towns along the western side of the sea.

Rebecca worked beside me, she on the belts and I on the sandals. Occasionally I would watch her small, strong hands as she cut the leather. She would gently bite her tongue in her precision. Her soft lips and smooth complexion were nearly perfect. Her eyes glistened when she talked. Heaven could be no better than living with Rebecca.

Soon after the second anniversary of our wedding, God blessed us with a baby girl. The name Mary sounded soft, so Rebecca and I agreed to call her

Mary. In time she grew to look just like her mother, beautiful inside and out.

Rebecca's closest friend was Salome, the wife of Zebedee and the mother of James and John. Salome lived in Capernaum, seven miles northeast of Magdala. Her husband and sons were commercial fishermen. Occasionally they would put in at Magdala to sell fish. When they did, they always shared the catch with my family. James and John were like older brothers to my daughter. They were the ones that first called her Mary Magdalene in order to distinguish her from the other Marys that they knew.

For years Rebecca suffered with seizures. The doctor told me he couldn't rid Rebecca of the demons that caused them. So four years ago Rebecca died. Following Rebecca's death, Salome came by more often to spend time with Mary Magdalene talking with her as a mother would to a daughter. Two years ago my daughter had a brief seizure, and I asked Jehovah to heal her as I had for Rebecca. This time I sensed an answer—be patient.

As time went on, James and John came less often as they were spending time with Jesus. I had heard that Jesus had healed many people, so I asked James if Jesus could come and heal Mary Magdalene of her seizures.

A few weeks later, a visitor entered my cobbler shop. Mary Magdalene asked if she could help him, and He introduced himself saying, "My name is Jesus."

I stopped my work to look at Him a little more closely. He was a large man with powerful shoulders and arms, yet He seemed gentle in composure. His eyes captured my attention when they met with my daughter's. They were intense yet kind.

"James and John asked me to come," He said quietly.

"I'm so glad you have," Mary said, "They told me you could heal me."

"And you Mary, what do you believe?"

Mary looked down then up. Her eyes settled on His as she nodded her head, "Yes." Then Jesus, with a heart full of compassion, commanded the demons to come out.

Mary Magdalene's body quivered, not once, but seven times as the demons left. She stood relaxed for a moment. Then with complete abandonment, she threw her arms around the neck of Jesus to thank Him.

After that, Mary Magdalene wasn't home quite as much, as she traveled with a group of women who served Jesus. When spring arrived she told me that Jesus was going to go to Jerusalem for the Passover. She was worried about His safety and wanted to go with Salome to minister to Him while He was there.

I told her, "If you feel in your heart that you should go, then you and He will be in my prayers daily."

So one morning she joined the small band of disciples headed for Jerusalem. Each day was lonely for me. It just wasn't the same around the shop without her. I think I missed her enthusiasm most.

Ten days had passed when she returned with Salome. Salome was unable to stay as she had to reach Capernaum by sundown. After Salome had left, I asked what had happened to their friend Jesus.

"Oh, Father, it was awful. The Pharisees had the Romans crucify him. I was so glad I was able to be there with Him. I stayed until He died and was placed in a tomb. The next day was the Sabbath. Before light on the third day, I went to the tomb with spices. When I got there I saw that the stone was rolled away."

"Was Jesus in the tomb?"

"No, when I looked in the tomb and saw that His body was gone I began to cry. In His place sat two angels, and they asked me, 'Why are you weeping?' 'They have taken away my Lord,' I said. Then when I turned, I saw Jesus, but I didn't know it was Jesus until He called me by name. Then I knew it was Him. His voice was gentle, but His eyes were firm when He said, 'Tell my disciples that I have risen.'"

"Did you tell them?"

"I tried to but they wouldn't believe me."

It was then that I took my daughter in my arms as I could feel the pain she must have felt to have watched her friend suffer and die. Tears flowed down my cheeks. The last time I had shed tears was at the death of Rebecca.

Mary, sensing my pain, reminded me that Rebecca had always believed in the coming Messiah and that now, since His death, she too would finally meet Him. Her words of encouragement brought me comfort and deep down inside I knew she was right especially when she said the last words He spoke to her were, "I shall ascend to My Father and your Father, to My God and your God."

Based on Matthew 27:56; Mark 16; Luke 8; John 20.

Joanna: A Financial Supporter of Jesus' Ministry

*M*y name is Joanna. I live in Tiberius on the west side of the Sea of Galilee with my husband, Chuza. My home while growing up was in Bethsaida, where my closest friends were Salome and Rebecca. Since all of us had a traditional upbringing our parents insisted on arranging our marriages. Salome's parents found her a young man whose father was a successful commercial fisherman. Rebecca's parents chose a man about her age who had worked with his parents in a general merchandise shop. As for me, my father worked in financial management for the local Romans so he selected a man older than I who was employed in similar work.

Salome has two sons, James and John. Rebecca died when her daughter, Mary Magdalene, was only twelve years old. Since that time, Salome has taken Mary Magdalene under her wing and has been good to continue to spend time with her during these last four years.

My husband, Chuza, worked at one time as business manager for the centurion who was the leader of the Roman Century stationed in Capernaum. When Herod the Great died, his son, Herod Antipas, was appointed by the Romans as Tetrarch of Galilee, and Pontius Pilate was made governor of Judea. Then Herod Antipas, who was building the city of Tiberius south of Capernaum, asked that Chuza become his business manager.

When Salome and I met in Magdala with Rebecca's daughter, Mary Magdalene, not long ago to catch up on family news, Salome shared that her sons James and John had joined an itinerant preacher named Jesus, who, with His apostles, had been traveling all around Galilee healing the sick and giving sight to the blind. He even healed Mary Magdalene of her seizures when He came to visit her and her father in their cobbler shop.

I was intrigued by what I was hearing about Jesus and decided I must find a way to meet Him. When Salome said that Jesus was preaching in Capernaum, I suggested that the three of us go there to hear Him.

We wrapped a few things in a carrying cloth and set out on our two hour journey. In Capernaum, we went directly to the synagogue and slipped into the back row where we could hear Jesus telling stories. Each story had a message. After the service John sought us out and asked if we would like to speak to Jesus.

In unison, our response was, "Yes!"

When we stood beside Jesus, He greeted each of us individually. He told Salome how grateful He was for the help of her reliable sons, James and John. Then He turned to Mary Magdalene. He studied her face for several moments as if to see how she was feeling before telling her to give His best wishes to her father. I think He cares a great deal for her.

Next Jesus turned to me and spoke with a smile, "You must be Joanna. Salome has told me all about you and your lifelong friendship."

"Yes, our friendship as young girls has only grown stronger over the years."

Since others were waiting to talk to Jesus, we soon moved outside to continue our conversation. Eventually Salome asked her son, James, if we could spend the night at his place. He was happy to hear we were staying over and said that he and John would love to have us so we would have some time to visit.

The five of us talked late into the night. As I listened to James and John tell about Jesus' traveling ministry, I sensed a need for some women to join the entourage so that meals would be prepared and clothes mended.

The next morning, after James and John had left, I told the other two women that I would like to travel with Jesus to prepare food for Him and His apostles because His healing ministry seemed so important. Salome and Mary Magdalene said they too would like to be of service in this way as well. Then I went on to explain that my husband, Chuza, in his job as business manager for Herod, had funds which were to be given to Jewish groups to mollify the Jews and hold down rebellion and that we could use some of this money to purchase food.

When we told Jesus about our idea, He gladly received it. So for the next year and a half, the three of us were a part of Jesus' itinerant ministry. We returned regularly to our homes, but after short stays, we would be off on another preaching and healing mission.

During our second spring together, we followed Jesus and the apostles to Jerusalem, but I was not prepared for what happened. The high priest, Caiaphas, had stirred up a mob of people in order to convince Pilot to crucify Jesus.

The women from Galilee stood with me at a distance weeping as we watched the crucifixion. I wanted to hide my face in my hands to lessen my pain, but I held my head high in loyalty to share His pain. After Jesus died, Joseph of Arimathea took His body down from the cross. We followed him to see the tomb where our Lord would be laid then returned to the inn and prepared spices and perfume to anoint His body. The next day was the Sabbath, so we rested in accordance with the commandment.

On the following day, at early dawn, we gathered our spices and perfume and walked the path to the burial site. Even though Joseph and Nicodemus had put some spices on Jesus' body, more were needed. Before we left we were somewhat concerned about the large stone that sealed the tomb, but this did not deter us from going. To our amazement, as we came close, we could see that the rock had been rolled away. When I looked into the open tomb, I saw two men in dazzling clothes. I was terrified and bowed my face to the ground. One of the men spoke, "Why do you seek the living among the dead? He is not here; He has risen!"

When we realized that He had indeed risen as He had said He would, Mary Magdalene, the other women, and I ran to tell Peter and the disciples. Peter was the only one who half believed, so he took off running to the tomb. But the rest of the disciples didn't even half believe.

When I returned to my home in Bethsaida, I was in good spirits, for I knew in my heart that Jesus had indeed risen from the dead and was all He had claimed to be. Eventually we received word that the disciples also believed, but it was only after Jesus had appeared to them behind closed doors. I guess they had to see for themselves before they were able to believe. As for me, I was grateful that Jesus allowed the three of us women, who had served Him so diligently, to be the first to believe in His resurrection and to spread the good news.

Based on Luke 8:2-3, 23:49 to 24:12.

Amasa: A Faithful Shepherd

*M*y name is Amasa. My father tended sheep all his life, as did his father, in the hill country south of Jerusalem. Even now my father, brothers, uncles, and cousins still herd sheep throughout the territory of our ancestors. Today my seven-year-old son, Eli, is going with me into Jerusalem to deliver some sheep to a buyer. Eli has been with me in the fields since the age of four. He loves the sheep and the sheep love him. Wherever he goes they go.

This morning Eli and I gathered the six sheep for our walk into the city. Danielle, my wife, was the first to rise. She let the younger children sleep while she prepared our breakfast. As Eli and I ate, she wrapped food in a carrying cloth for our lunch on the road. She gave each of us a warm hug as we headed north on the trail. Her eyes were moist because this was the first time her young son was going on such a long journey.

As we herded our sheep along the hillside, the sky grew brighter and brighter until there was full daylight. The hills were already turning green although it was early in the spring. We had been on the road several hours when we reached the outskirts of Jerusalem where we came to a public well. I turned and asked Eli, "Would you like to rest awhile? We can draw some water and see what your mother has packed for our lunch."

"Yes, I am hungry."

Eli would never admit it, but I knew he must also be tired. We chose some flat rocks on a south slope that was greener than the rest. The sheep grazed close by as Eli opened the carrying cloth. Inside were figs, dried mutton, and honey-sweetened bread. Of the seven figs, Eli offered me four, and he pulled three to his side of the cloth. With his small hands, he passed me some mutton and bread. Eli watched his grazing sheep while I watched Eli.

The road was filled with travelers on this day following the Sabbath. People were preparing for the Passover which would take place in six more days. I had nearly finished my lunch when I saw a crowd gathering around a man riding on a donkey's colt. The people were laying branches in the path where the colt would walk. As the man riding the young donkey came closer, I could hear the crowd chanting, "Hosanna to the Son of David! Blessed is He who comes in the name of the Lord! Hosanna in the highest!"

I walked up to a woman who was drawing water at the well to ask, "Who is the man on the colt?"

"That is Jesus, the Messiah."

By now I had forgotten about the sheep. Eli joined me and I held his hand tightly as I intently watched Jesus ride by us. Jesus' kind eyes met mine as He passed by. Though no words were spoken, I felt I knew this man and believed that truly He was our promised Messiah.

The crowd pushed on past. Soon just Eli, the sheep, and I remained. As Eli started to gather the sheep, I said, "Let's sit awhile longer. I want to share a story with you that I have never told anyone before."

Eli, sensing the serious tone of my voice, sat down, forgetting his beloved sheep.

"Eli, when I was just your age, I was in the field one winter night with my father and the sheep when suddenly an angel of the Lord stood before us."

"An angel of the Lord? What did he look like? Were you afraid?"

"I was very frightened, but I pretended to be brave. The angel said, 'Today in the city of David there has been born a Savior Who is Christ the Lord. You will find the baby wrapped in cloths and lying in a manger.' As soon as he finished, the sky was filled with the heavenly host singing, 'Glory to God in the highest, and on earth peace, good will toward men.'"

"What happened next? Why did the angels sing such a song?"

"My father took me by the hand, and together with the other shepherds, we went to the town of Bethlehem to look for the child in the manger."

"Were you able to find him?"

"Yes, we walked directly to a stable behind the inn, and all of the shepherds knelt down out of respect for the baby who was sleeping there. As everyone knelt, my father turned loose of my hand. I wasn't tall enough to see the baby from where my father was kneeling, so I walked right up beside the manger and looked in."

"What did He look like?"

"A little like your baby brother when he was first born."

"How did you know it was the baby the angel told you about?"

"When I turned to look at the baby's mother, she was smiling at me, so I asked, 'The angels told my father and the rest of the shepherds that your baby is our Savior. Is that true?' The baby's mother pulled me close to her and spoke in a soft voice just to me, 'Yes, many months ago at my home in Nazareth, an angel told me I would have a son who would be known as the Son of God.' I then asked her what was the name of her baby? She answered, 'The angel told me to call Him Jesus.' It was then that I felt the crook of my father's staff around my leg nudging me to return to his side. I have never shared my story with anyone because I didn't want it disputed. From that day until this, thirty-three years have come and gone, but I have never forgotten the baby's name nor His face. Now today, more then ever before, I believe the words of the angels who said that Jesus will be our Savior."

With his hand reaching for mine, Eli said, "Oh, father, let's gather our sheep and follow Jesus into Jerusalem."

And so we did, and we went.

Based on Matthew 21:1-11; Luke 2:7-20; Luke 1:26-33.

Adlai: A Lawyer

*M*y name is Adlai. This past spring I turned sixteen and, at the same time, graduated from the academy for Pharisees. Most Jewish boys are in the synagogue school through their twelfth year. I had always wanted to be a Pharisee and a lawyer like my father and grandfather, so I studied hard all through school in order to be accepted into the academy.

For the last four years, I have studied the scrolls of the Pentateuch and the prophets and the addendum to the Law. The first two studies were interesting. The addendum to Moses' Law was boring to me because I thought the authors had created the Law for the trivial things of life. I kept this boredom to myself, of course, since I was a Pharisee and wanted to be considered an expert in the Law. So I memorized the addendum to the Law with the same fervor that I performed all of the tasks assigned to me. Lest one think I am not a respecter of the Law, let me hasten to say that the basic Jewish Law is, and always has been, essential to our survival as God's people.

Even before my study at the academy, my father and grandfather had told me about the importance of the Jewish religion and the Jewish Law. Our religion has been the source of our Law. Throughout Jewish history our survival as a people has depended on our religion and our Law, rather than any territory the Jews may have held. The tie between our religion and our Law was why I wanted to be a lawyer among the Pharisees and continue my family's tradition.

During my upperclassman years at the academy, I would go with other students into the area around the temple, where we would discuss the Law with anyone who would enter into a debate with us. I would often try to get a Sadducee and a Pharisee to debate each other. I always secretly enjoyed a good altercation. The Sadducees doubted immortality and accepted only the Torah, the written Law as found in the Pentateuch. The Pharisees, on the other hand, believed in life after death and in adding details to the written Law. Over the years the Pharisees had added thousands of laws, most of which seemed trivial to me.

On this spring day a group of recent law graduates had gathered near the temple. Everyone was talking about the teacher from Galilee named Jesus who entered Jerusalem two days ago riding a donkey. The crowd had placed leafy branches all along the road in His path and exclaimed, "Hosanna, blessed is He who comes in the name of the Lord."

I wondered about this Jesus who claimed to be the Son of God. We heard that He had just subdued the Sadducees with His reply to their question about life after death. Since I had been the leader of my class at the academy, I was elected to approach Jesus where He sat on a large rock and ask Him a question we had all been wondering about, "Teacher, which is the greatest commandment in the Law?" My eyes met those of Jesus as He began to speak, "You shall love the Lord your God with all your heart, and with all your soul, and with all your mind. And a second is like it, you shall love your neighbor as yourself. On these two commandments depend all the Law and the teaching of the prophets."

There was something about the tone of His voice that carried with it a sense of final authority. Even though I had spent years studying the Law, I had never thought of it in quite that way before. The rest of the commandments do follow naturally from these two, and the Pharisees' addendum to the Law could be thrown out, as I secretly had suspected all the time. His words were so simple yet so true that I decided to take it one step further and ask Him another question, "Who is my neighbor?"

Then Jesus paused and looked me squarely in the face then leaned back and began to tell me a story about a Jewish man traveling from Jerusalem to Jericho who was beaten by robbers and left for dead. Three men in turn came along: a priest, a Levite, and a Samaritan. The first two walked by on the other side of the road while only the Samaritan stopped to help the injured man.

With his eyes still fixed on mine, Jesus asked, "Which one was a neighbor?"

"Of course," I quietly answered, "the one who showed mercy towards the man."

Then He leaned forward and said, "Go and do likewise."

When He stood to his feet, another one of the Pharisees approached Him. As He turned to walk with him in the midst of the crowd, His words continued to echo through my mind, "Go and do likewise. Go and do likewise."

Then I thought of all those in my community and even those not so bright in my class whom I had considered inferior to me and not worthy of my love. I knew I had been wrong in thinking of them in this way. I had always determined to be an expert in the Law. Now I was instead to become a master of love—for both God and for man. From this day forth, I will go and do likewise.

Based on Matthew 22:34-40; Mark 12:28-31; Luke 10:25-37; Deuteronomy 6:5; Leviticus 19:18.

Simon of Cyrene: Picked Out of the Crowd

J left Judea as a young man in quest of fame and fortune to settle in Cyrene overlooking the Mediterranean on the northern edge of Africa (eastern Libya). I am now fifteen years older and a little wiser. I have given up on fame, having found what is truly important—a wife, Angela, and two sons, Alexander, age ten, and Rufus, age eight.

Angela's family came to Cyrene from Greece to grow silphium, a medicinal herb that has been in much demand. After Angela and I were married, I joined the family business as a trader, and now travel to Rome, Athens, Alexandria, and Jerusalem to sell silphium to the local shopkeepers in those cities.

Spring has arrived, and I am needing to make a trip to Jerusalem. When I told Angela, she asked, "Simon, why don't you take Alexander, Rufus, and me with you to Jerusalem? The Mediterranean is never more blue than during the calm days of spring."

"What about school?", I protested halfheartedly.

"I'll take along the Hebrew scrolls so the boys can study aboard ship. In Jerusalem they can practice speaking Hebrew with the shopkeepers you call on. Just think of the history they can learn in such an ancient city."

As you might have guessed, I gave in. Travel would be a little slower, I suppose, but, then again, it won't be quite so lonely.

So with that we were off, and our journey to Jerusalem had begun. After three weeks at sea with only a stop at Alexandria, we landed at the port of Caesarea near Jerusalem. From my previous trips to Jerusalem, I was familiar with several inns that could house my family. Angela picked the one she liked best. One afternoon we decided to visit the temple. All four of us stood beside Solomon's Porch gawking up at the top of the temple, one hundred and fifty feet above. My sons had never seen such an impressive structure. Those passing by could easily tell that we were from the country.

On Friday morning, I awoke before Angela and the boys. This was to be our last day in Jerusalem before returning home. On the previous days, we had toured the historic sites and spent quite a bit of time in the marketplace, where I sold my silphium, but today we would climb Golgotha Hill and get a panoramic view of the city. It was a sight I just knew the boys would remember forever.

It was still before the hour of nine when we began our climb. There seemed to be an unusually large number of people out, and I wondered why the path was so crowded. Looking back over the heads of the crowd, I could see a man who had been severely lashed and beaten. Angela heard me gasp when He stumbled as He tried to carry the heavy crossbeam for a cross. Out of sheer fright, she tightly gripped the hands of Alexander and Rufus. I was glad they were still small enough not to be able to see over the heads of those around them.

As the Roman soldier scanned the crowd, he fixed his eyes on mine, "You there, carry the cross!," he bellowed.

Quickly I glanced at Angela, but I knew what I must do. Terror struck her eyes as I stepped out of the crowd.

The soldier motioned for me to bend down then placed the heavy cross-beam on my shoulder. As I trudged forward, the crowds taunted the man I was carrying the cross for. Some even spit in His face. Others called out His name—Jesus. Then I wondered to myself, "What could He have done to have deserved such a horrible fate?"

When we reached the top of the hill, the Roman soldiers lifted the cross-beam from my shoulder and laid it on the ground next to a plaque that read, "King of the Jews." My heart pounded in my throat, as much from fear as from the heavy load. I wanted to rush back to find my family, but something held me captive as I looked into the face of this "King of the Jews." His body was beaten and bruised. In places, it was even bleeding. He didn't look like a king, but when He fixed His eyes on mine and said, "Thank you, Simon," I knew that He was no ordinary man.

Based on Mark 15-21.

Judd: A Criminal

*M*y name is Judd. Today I am seen as a criminal, but it was not always so. As a boy, I grew up in Apollonia, which is forty miles northwest of Jerusalem or twenty-two miles south of Caesarea Maritima on the Mediterranean coast. My people are Samaritans. From my early youth, I sailed on small boats in the Mediterranean off of Apollonia. At the age of twelve, I sailed with my father on a Roman cargo ship out of Caesarea Maritima bound for Alexandria, Egypt. When I saw the men hoist the sails and felt the ocean spray against my brow, I knew I was where I belonged.

By the age of sixteen I was a first mate sailing regularly out of Caesarea Maritima for Rome, Athens, Tarsus, Alexandria, and Ephesus. After a month or two at sea, I would return to Apollonia for an extended stay.

Amaris was the prettiest girl in our town and fun to be around. We had always been friends, so I can't really say when we fell in love. When we both reached the age of sixteen, we asked for our parents' permission to marry. Amaris knew my work meant I would be gone for a month or more at a time, but we each believed that our love could hold us together throughout the times of separation.

Adam was our first child, then two years later Adam's brother, Zared, was born.

Our boys were ten and twelve when I had an accident at sea. A rope for loosening the sails entangled my left hand and maimed it. For the rest of the trip I was of no help in running the ship. When we reached our home port, Caesarea Maritima, a doctor told me I would never be able to use my left hand again. This, of course, ended my sailing career.

Usually the twenty-two mile journey home was sheer joy, knowing I would soon be with Amaris, Adam, and Zared. But this time I felt a heaviness in my step as I knew that life would never be the same again for them or for me.

When I reached home, my greatest supporters, Amaris, Adam, and Zared ran to the door to greet me. With a little bit of embarrassment, I told them about the accident at sea. Adam and Zared sat on my lap and laid their heads against my chest while Amaris gave me the encouragement I needed to go forward. I knew they understood.

So at sunup the next day, I began my search for another job. My hand was still hurting but my self-esteem was hurting even more, for my self-esteem had always been equated with success at my job. After several weeks, I concluded there were no openings in Apollonia nor in the surrounding countryside. Each time I applied for work, I could see the prospective employer looking at my bad hand as he shook his head, "No."

After a month of disappointments, I suggested to Amaris that we go to Jerusalem. Such a large city would surely have jobs for a willing worker. The next day before sunrise the four of us put our belongings in a cart behind our donkey and headed for Jerusalem. Adam refused to ride because he was a man, but Zared agreed to a turn in the cart after his mother had ridden for several miles.

After spending the night in Lydda, the halfway point, we departed early for Jerusalem. When we arrived in Jerusalem the streets were jammed with people scurrying about. Amaris and I kept looking for a place to set up camp near some water. With the mild spring weather, we could live out of our cart until I was able to find work. We walked all the way through Jerusalem without finding a place to stop, so we continued south for five more miles to Bethlehem.

By the time we arrived, the sun had set and the boys were tired. With both determination and apprehension, I knocked on the door of an inn. To my relief, I was greeted by a jovial man who said, "My name is Bartholomew. How may I help you?"

"I am Judd. My family and I have journeyed from Apollonia in Samaria. I'll have no money until I find work. I am looking for a place where I can get water, park my cart for the evening, and bed down my family."

"My rooms are a denarius for the night, but you may stay free in the stable behind the house. You'll find water and clean straw where you can make a bed for your family."

Bartholomew went with us behind the inn to the covered stable. He helped unhitch the donkey and showed me a railing which could be used to hold the cart level. As Bartholomew turned to go he said, "After you water your donkey, you can put him in the pen with the other animals."

Amaris spoke to Adam and Zared, "Help me look for wood scraps to make a fire for supper." As they began to search in the darkening dusk, a robust woman came around the corner carrying a large bowl.

"My name is Abigail. I'm Bartholomew's wife. He told me about your long trip. This stew was left over after I had served all my guests for supper. Let me fill your bowls."

"I am Judd, and this is Amaris, Adam, and Zared. May Jehovah bless you for your kindness, but you must know that I have always provided for my family, and I shall continue to do so as soon as I find work."

For eight straight days, except for the Sabbath, I looked for a job in Jerusalem and the surrounding area. My rejections always came as soon as the prospective employer noticed my useless left hand. Bartholomew continued to let us stay at his stable. Even though I told Amaris we were not to take charity, I could tell that Abigail was replenishing our dwindling staples.

Late in the evening Bartholomew would stop by to offer encouragement. He even told me how happy Abigail was. She had never been able to have children and seemed to have adopted Amaris as her daughter and Adam and Zared as her grandsons.

On the ninth day of imposing on Bartholomew and Abigail, I made a mistake that would cost me all that I had. Because Moses was my ancestor, I had learned the ten commandments as a boy, just like the Judeans. But this one day I was particularly hungry, and as I walked through the market square at the end of the day, I passed an unattended booth where the remains of the day's vegetables lay. I rationalized to myself, "These will be thrown out later tonight, so I'll just help take them off of their hands."

As I walked through the marketplace, a group of Judean men apprehended me. I felt guilty and ashamed when they took the vegetables out of my pouch and ushered me straight to the prison where they told the guard about my stealing. To my dismay, I found that a Samaritan can be put to death in Judea for stealing from a Jew. Since the day I had sailed on a Roman cargo ship as a twelve-year-old, I had never known a moment of fear. Now I was frightened and scared. What would happen to Amaris, Adam, and Zared?

On the third day of my imprisonment, Bartholomew found me. He said, "We have all been worried about you. Abigail insisted on moving your family into our quarters when you didn't return. Amaris was terrified at first but is now doing better as she can see how the boys love their adoptive grandmother. We will make sure your boys are fed, clothed, and loved."

As he left, Bartholomew and I agreed to hope for the best. The jail held several other criminals. One of these was Barabbas, who said that Pontius Pilate, Procurator of Judea, would release a criminal of choice to the Jews for Passover. Barabbas was getting his friends to bring their friends to improve his chances of being chosen. I secretly hoped I might be selected for release because of my lesser infraction.

But Barabbas' politics worked, and he was freed. The next day, another criminal and I were taken from the prison to Golgatha Hill where criminals were crucified. We were joined by a third whom they called Jesus. Jesus was more mistreated than I by the crowd. The guard told me that Jesus claimed to be the Son of God and that Pilate himself had ordered a sign to be nailed on His cross that read, "This Is the King of the Jews." Amidst His abuse, Jesus said, "Father, forgive them; for they do not know what they are doing."

As the three of us hung side by side on our crosses, the man on the far side screamed and cursed in his pain while this One, whom they called Jesus, cried out to His Heavenly Father. His profound submission convinced me that His claim to be the Son of God must be true, so with all the breath left in me I said, "Jesus, remember me when you come into your kingdom."

And He answered, "Truly I say to you, today you shall be with Me in Paradise."

Based on Luke 23:32-43.

Marcellus: A Soldier Set Free

My name is Marcellus. As a boy growing up, I lived in Croton on the southern edge of Italy. My sister, Adoria, is four years older than I, and my brother, Sextus, is eight years older. The three of us were always close despite our age differences. My father, a fisherman, had hoped that Sextus would join him in his fishing business, but Sextus had his heart set on becoming a legionnaire. As soon as he was old enough he signed up with the army. Adoria married when she was fifteen and has a son and a daughter. Whenever I would visit the children, they would always run to greet me and give me the biggest hug ever. Of course, I couldn't resist and would sweep them off their feet to give them a big squeeze back.

I had always wanted to be just like my big brother, so when I reached the age of sixteen, I joined the Roman Legion also. After three months of training in Italy, I boarded a ship to join the Roman Garrison in Jerusalem. I had been on the sea helping my father with his fishing boats since my early boyhood so traveling across the Mediterranean was an exciting adventure for me. After landing in Caesarea Maritima, I traveled to Jerusalem to find my Roman Cohort where I would join five hundred other fellow legionnaires.

Twenty years have come and gone and I am still serving my country. After ten years in Jerusalem I was promoted to sergeant and transferred to the century in Capernaum. I decided to celebrate my tenth anniversary of duty in

Capernaum with a visit to the marketplace to mingle with the people. I thought I might find a little something for the children of my niece and nephew. Even though my sister's children are grown now, I still think of them often. Sometimes I think maybe I should have had a wife and children of my own. Then again, maybe not, as my life in the military may have been too hard on them.

When I arrived at the marketplace, it was crowded since the fishermen had just unloaded their day's catch into wooden bins. Women selling figs were under the shade of their makeshift booths and they cried out to me to buy as I passed. A blind man, who was also crippled, sat alone on a flat rock alongside of a fruit stand waving his cup in the air. I stopped to buy some grapes then placed the change I had received in his cup. The sound of the coins in his cup brought a smile to his face and to mine.

I hadn't seen exactly what I wanted to buy for my niece and nephew's children, but I kept looking. In the shops were carved wooden whistles, small earthen vessels, and beautiful sashes. Since many of the women were wearing the sashes, I picked out one made of purple for my niece's daughter and carefully folded it to fit in the fold of my garment. I couldn't decide on what to get my nephew's son, and then I saw the perfect gift. It was a leather string with a medallion of two nails bent in the shape of a cross. I bargained a little with the man in the booth until we settled on a fair price, then I placed it in the fold of my garment along with the purple sash.

By this time, the sun was high in the mid-day sky, and I was hungry. So I began making my way towards a large fruit stand away from the shore line. As I pushed my way through the crowds buying fish out of the wooden bins, I felt a tug on the sash around my waist. I reached for my money pouch, but it was too late. It was gone.

When I turned, I saw a young boy quickly making his way through the crowd. Thinking it was he who stole my pouch, I stopped him and shook him, demanding that he give me back my money. But he acted like he didn't know what I was talking about and lifted his hands. People were looking at me now, wondering why I was shaking him so. He looked innocent enough, so I let him go. At least I still had the gifts.

Needing a drink of water, I headed toward the well. A man, older than I, was at the well drawing up some water in a bucket. As I neared he offered me a cup of water. As thirsty as I was, I accepted. Then he spoke, "My name is Andrew, and I saw you shaking that boy."

"My name is Marcellus. Yes, I thought he was the one who had just stolen my money pouch. But he looked so innocent and lifted his hands to the sky, so I figured that maybe I was mistaken. I was hoping to get a couple of pieces of fruit before heading back to the quarters, but now I'm just glad for a cool drink of water."

"Would you care to have some of my lunch? I have more than I can possibly eat."

Normally I would not have accepted such an offer, but Andrew had such a friendly manner that I could hardly turn it down. He motioned for me to sit with him under the shade of a nearby olive tree where he opened his cloth wrap and handed me half his bread and cheese. We were both hungry, so at first we quietly ate. Something about the good food improved my disposition, so I asked, "Andrew, tell me about yourself."

"I do some fishing with my father, but I spend most of my time with the Christian churches in Galilee."

My heart began to race as I asked, "Are you a follower of Jesus the Christ?"

"Yes, I was one of His twelve apostles when He began His ministry."

My first impulse was to somehow excuse myself and leave, but Andrew seemed so sincere that I decided to stay and tell this apostle about my encounter with Jesus twenty years ago. Haltingly I began my confession, "I was a part of the Roman cohort that took Jesus to the Praetorium where Pilot sentenced Him to be crucified."

"You soldiers were very cruel to my dearest friend."

"Yes, that is true. I wanted to be like the seasoned soldiers, so as they began to mock Jesus and beat Him and spit on Him, I, too, spit in His face."

There was a moment of silence as Andrew looked away, but I had to tell someone what I had done, so I continued, "After I spit, I thought about my brother, Sextus, and my sister, Adoria. If either had known, they would have been appalled. Then I felt so embarrassed and so ashamed. Still I followed along to Golgatha as one of the soldiers who would control the crowd for the crucifixion. My feelings of guilt increased as Jesus hung on the cross. Instead of lashing out at those tormenting Him, He said, 'Father, forgive them; for they know not what they do.'"

After a moment of silence Andrew said, "Jesus would have forgiven you too, for that is who He is."

"I'm not sure I understand how He could do that, but you must help me, for the sorrow I have felt since that day is breaking my heart."

Andrew didn't say anything right away, but when he turned his face towards me, I saw compassion, not hatred, in his eyes, and he said, "Marcellus, there is forgiveness if you are willing to confess your sins and believe that Jesus is the Son of God."

"You have heard my confession, and I do believe."

"Marcellus, this day your sins are forgiven."

His words echoed through my mind, "This day your sins are forgiven." Then I remembered, these were the words of Jesus twenty years ago. Finally I was able to receive the forgiveness that He offered me and it was because of Andrew that I understood.

Based on Matthew 27:27-31; Mark 15:16-20; Luke 23:34.

Joseph of Arimathea: A Secret Disciple of Jesus

*M*y name is Joseph and I live in Arimathea, a small village between Jerusalem and Joppa. This has been my family's home for many generations. The peace and quiet of Arimathea soothes my spirit when I return home from work in the city. My fleet of trading ships operates out of Joppa and sails to ports throughout the Mediterranean. I also have small living quarters in Jerusalem and Joppa since I am in these cities on business nearly every week.

My financial success entitles me to a prominent position on the seventy-one member Sanhedrin, the Great Council of Elders of Israel. This body meets regularly in the Hall of Gazith in the temple in Jerusalem to deal with matters affecting the Jewish people. The Romans, very wisely, let us Jews govern ourselves as long as we pay the Roman taxes. Politics drives much of the council's actions, but I always seek justice for my people.

The latest discussions in the council have centered around a Galilean preacher named Jesus who has been coming to Jerusalem from Capernaum to teach. On one of Jesus' early visits to the temple, He drove out the money-changers. In my heart I knew He was right but most of the Pharisees vowed to kill Him because He was destroying a business vital to their financial well-being.

After that day, I became a secret disciple of Jesus. If the other Pharisees knew of my belief in Jesus, I feared they might throw me off of the council. But if I remained a member, I felt that I could be of some help to Jesus.

Well, I was wrong. Caiaphas, the Chief Priest, was fearful that Jesus would one day gain enough authority among the people that his position would be usurped and given to Jesus. He grew jealous day by day and was determined to have Jesus crucified. My heart was broken when I found that my every effort to intervene on Jesus' behalf was thwarted by Caiaphas. My sadness was intensified as I watched His cruel crucifixion knowing that He was innocent and didn't deserve to die. The injustice of it all enraged me.

Not long ago I had purchased some space in a garden near Golgotha Hill and had commissioned a tomb to be hewn from the rock since I was nearing the age when one must think of such things. After they had pierced His side as He hung on the cross, I wondered about the possibility of taking Jesus' body down from the cross so He could have a decent burial. The guards said that I would have to check with Pilate.

Over the years I had had many dealings with Pilate since my ships were sometimes under contract to his government for hauling supplies between Caesarea Maritima and Rome. So I called on Pilate once again, but this time I found a beaten and despondent man. When I asked him if I could bury Jesus, he muttered to himself, "If only I had listened to my wife instead of the mob." Then he checked with his centurion to be sure Jesus was dead and granted my request.

Another Pharisee, Nicodemus, who was also a secret disciple of Jesus, purchased a hundred pound mixture of myrrh and aloe for the preservation of the body, and I bought a fine linen cloth to wrap Jesus with. Together Nicodemus and I wrapped Jesus' body with the spices and placed it in the unused tomb. While we worked, Mary Magdalene and Mary, the mother of Joses, watched through tear-stained eyes. After the body was placed in the tomb, I paid six strong men to seal the entrance with a large rock.

As they were rolling the rock across the entrance, I found a seat in the garden. My whole body went limp from exhaustion and discouragement. I had done about as much as I could for this One I had come to love and respect. Still, the inevitable had come to pass. Now, this agonizing day was over and I felt like life was over too. My hoped-for Messiah was dead. Some of his disciples said He would arise from the dead, but how probable could that be?

Still feeling guilty for not having been able to prevent this crime from taking place, I wondered how I would be able to forgive myself. It was then that I remembered the words that Jesus cried out to His Father even while He was on the cross, "Father, forgive them; for they know not what they do." When I looked back at the tomb, the last rays of light from the closing dusk spilled over the large rock sealing the entrance, and I wondered to myself, "Could anything good come from the death of this innocent man?"

Based on Matthew 27:57-61; Mark 15:42-47; Luke 23:34,50-56;
John 19:38-42; Matthew 21:12, 27:19.

Cleopas: A Man from Emmaus

*M*y name is Cleopas. I am an innkeeper in Emmaus. My business has been good for many years because of my location just off the main road from Jerusalem to Joppa on the Mediterranean Sea. Many travelers, coming from the coast, stop at my inn for the night then leave early the next morning for their business in Jerusalem.

My wife Mary and I regularly attend the local synagogue to worship Jehovah. Several months ago, an itinerant preacher named Jesus spoke at our synagogue. He read to us from our scroll of the prophet Isaiah. When He finished, He returned the scroll to the attendant and sat down. The eyes of everyone in the synagogue were fixed on Jesus. From where He sat with His face in full view, He spoke where all could hear, "Today this Scripture has been fulfilled in your hearing."

Not all believed, but it was clear to me that Jesus was the long-awaited Messiah. Mary also believed. Over the next several months, when travelers returning from Jerusalem would tell us that Jesus was in Jerusalem, Mary and I would go there to listen to Him teach. Soon Mary and I were telling all of our customers about Jesus and His teachings. Many were more interested in business; still, the number of followers increased as we shared our faith in Jesus.

On a Thursday near the spring equinox, I felt mysteriously drawn to Jerusalem. When I shared my feelings with Mary, she explained that she too had heard a small voice from within calling her to Jerusalem. The next morning, well before sunrise, we left so we would reach the city early in the morning. As we arrived in Jerusalem, we came upon a great crowd moving through the city to a hill on the outskirts of town and we followed along.

Anguish overcame me as I could see that the Roman soldiers were preparing to crucify the Jesus we had come to know and love. When the soldiers nailed the spikes into Jesus' hands, I couldn't bear to look. Mary gasped then began to silently sob. I tried my best to comfort her, but I was in such a state of shock that I was of little help. We stayed at the cross until Jesus took His last breath.

Normally Mary and I would have returned to Emmaus the same evening because of the needs of our business, but this time the Spirit spoke to us saying we should stay two nights with the other disciples. For most of the next day, we prayed with a large group of disciples for understanding. Our minds could not grasp why Jehovah would let our Messiah be crucified.

On the third day, after a morning of prayer with the group, Mary and I began our walk home to Emmaus. As we walked slowly along, discussing the events in Jerusalem, a stranger approached and asked, "May I walk along with you?"

"Yes, welcome."

"What are you two discussing, and why does it make you look so sad?"

Mary and I looked at each other then stood still for a moment before I said, "You must be the only person visiting Jerusalem who does not know about the crucifixion of Jesus."

All the way to Emmaus, we shared with the stranger the happenings and our desolate feelings from the loss of our Lord. He, in turn, shared Scriptures with us. When we reached our inn, we invited our new friend to come inside for a rest and a bite to eat before He went on His way.

Mary poured some wine and laid a loaf of her bread before our guest then joined us at the table. As soon as she sat down, our friend picked up the loaf, blessed it, and broke off a piece for Mary and one for me. With the breaking of the bread, a miracle happened. It was as if our eyes had been covered, and now we saw clearly. We knew now that it was indeed Jesus we had been speaking with, but as soon as we recognized Him, He vanished from our sight. I asked Mary, "Was your heart burning within you as was mine while He was speaking to us on the road about the Scriptures?"

Mary and I knew that we must return to Jerusalem immediately so we could search out the eleven apostles and tell them the good news of the resurrection of Jesus. This time our journey was swift, and our hearts were light. As we went down the road together, I felt as though I could walk forever. When I glanced over at Mary as she walked stride for stride with me, I could see the same joy on her face that had been there when Jesus broke the bread. Joy overflowed my heart too as I realized that I serve a risen Savior.

Based on Luke 24:13-35.

Thomas: The Doubter

*M*y name is Thomas. As a boy in my home town of Antioch, I attended morning classes at the synagogue and afternoon classes at the Greek school. My twin brother, Tobias, and I excelled in the math and science classes taught by the Greeks. We used these skills in the family boat-building business.

As I followed my father around the construction area as a boy, I would hear him say, "Measure it twice to get it right. Test it and test it again. I have to see it to believe it." My father's boats were the most seaworthy ones built because he demanded precision.

When I was fourteen my family moved to Capernaum where we continued in the boat-building business. Not long after Tobias' seventeenth birthday, he married and started a family. My brother and I remained close as we continued working with our father in the business. As Tobias gained stature as a family man, friends and customers referred to him as Tobias and to me as "The Twin."

Two of our good customers were Zebedee and Jonah. They were successful commercial fishermen. Jonah's sons, Simon and Andrew, and Zebedee's boys, James and John, were in the business with their fathers. The boys were close to my age and became my best friends.

At daybreak one fall day, I walked down to the shore where the fishermen kept their boats. I found Andrew busily mending his nets, so I stopped to ask, "Where have you been? As I have visited the fishermen in recent months, I haven't seen you."

Andrew put his net down then stood to talk. His countenance had always been warm and friendly, but today there was a special radiance on his face. In his quiet manner he began, "Simon and I have become apostles of Jesus. He has filled our lives with joy, and He'll do the same for you. Come, let's find Jesus so you can meet Him."

Based on what Andrew had said and what I had already heard about Jesus, I was curious to meet Him, so I went along. As we walked, I asked, "What has happened as you have spent time with Jesus?"

"Jesus has done many miraculous things. He removed an unclean spirit from a man. He healed Simon's mother-in-law Hannah of a fever. Another time He cleansed a leper. Even a paralyzed man regained full use of his arms and legs."

"Now that's hard to believe. I think I'd have to see it to believe it."

"Oh, you can see plenty of miracles, but you will have to spend time with Jesus."

"Where are we headed to find your friend?"

"Jesus rises before dawn and walks into the hills to pray. If we walk the path He normally takes, we should meet Him returning."

The sun had been up about an hour as we reached the foothills outside Capernaum. The dew, which still glistened in the sun, would soon be dried by the warmth of the clear blue sky. We had walked less than a mile when Andrew said, "That's Jesus coming this way."

In the distance I could see a man moving with a relaxed stride down the hill. He waved when He recognized Andrew. As soon as Jesus reached us, he placed His powerful hands on Andrew's shoulders and looked down into his eyes with a smile as He said, "So good to see you, Andrew."

Then Andrew put his arm around me and said, "Jesus, I want you to meet my close friend, Thomas. He and his father build our fishing boats."

"Thomas, you must be a skilled craftsman, for I have always felt very safe in rough waters in your boats."

I was glad then that my Father had been so insistent on good craftsmanship and felt proud to have trained under him all these years. Jesus continued to ask me about my family as we turned on the road that would take us to Capernaum. Andrew was quiet as the three of us walked, and Jesus explained to me how Andrew, Peter, James, and John had taken time from their fishing business to serve as His disciples. Jesus was more winsome than anyone I had ever met. Before we reached the shore of the lake, Jesus challenged me to follow Him as my four friends had, saying, "Building new lives is even more of a challenge than building fine boats."

"I've invested my life in my father's business, but what you've said today makes sense to me. It will be a risk and I know my father will be disappointed, but, yes, I want to follow you."

So that night I joined my friends as an apostle of Jesus. My family was surprised as this seemed so unlike me. I had always been so predictable and stable. Now I was leaving everyone and everything behind to follow someone I barely knew. I think in some ways I even surprised myself. But I had given my word, so I stuck with it, and I wasn't disappointed.

Even though Jesus was busy teaching and healing the multitudes, He found time to give special instruction to the twelve of us apostles. He told us to go out to the people of Israel to heal the sick so the people would believe He was the Son of God. Some of the other disciples had more success than I with this command. I tended to wait in the background and pray as they followed his words and healed the people.

For two years I listened to Jesus teaching as I was going to the towns and villages across Judea sharing His good news with the people. One late winter day, the warmth in the air foretold of spring on the way. A messenger, breathless from running, spoke to Jesus saying, "Martha and Mary need your help, for your good friend Lazarus is very sick."

After the messenger left, Jesus looked into my eyes as he said, "Lazarus is dead. I am glad for your sake that I was not there so that you may believe."

I was so moved by Jesus' persistent efforts to dismiss my doubts that I could hardly wait to see what He would do. As it turned out, Jesus spoke, and Lazarus was resurrected.

Several weeks later, before the feast of the Passover, Jesus gathered the twelve together and said, "I go to prepare a place for you." His eyes moved to mine as He continued, "And you know the way where I am going."

I felt confused about what He was saying and blurted out, "Lord, we do not know where you are going. How do we know the way?"

Calmly Jesus continued his instructions as if someday I would understand. Little did I expect that on the day before the Sabbath Jesus' words would be fulfilled. It was then that the men of the high priest, Caiaphas, dragged Jesus before Pilate where the mob successfully demanded crucifixion. When Jesus did not save himself, I and several other disciples hid out in a room behind closed doors in fear for our lives.

On the evening of the day after the Sabbath, I left the room to buy some food. When I returned, the others told me that Jesus had visited them. I said, "Unless I shall see the nail wounds in His hands, and put my fingers into the place of the nails, and put my hand into His side, I will not believe."

Eight days later, while meeting with others behind shut doors, Jesus appeared again. He wasn't a ghost as I had expected; instead, it was just as if He were alive again. When He appeared in the room, the first thing He said was, "Peace be with you." Then He moved over to me and extended His hands saying, "Place your fingers in the nail holes." When I did, He took my hand and placed it in the hole in his side as He said, "Thomas, I want you to believe."

When I pulled my hand out, the only words I could manage were, "My Lord and my God!"

To this very day people refer to me and those who doubt as a "Doubting Thomas." Such words are simply not true, for no one believes in Jesus, the Son of God, more fervently than I.

Based on John 11:14-16, 14:1-5, 20:24-28; Matthew 10:1-8.

Andrew: The Friendliest Disciple

$\mathcal{M}$y name is John. From my home in Tiberias, on the Sea of Galilee, I began the walk to Capernaum, a distance of ten miles. My father had asked me to deliver a payment to the collector of customs whose office was in this town.

An hour had passed when I stopped at the well in Gennesaret. A young man about my age had also stopped for a drink.

"Shalom."

"Shalom."

"Do I take the right fork ahead for Capernaum?"

"Yes. That's where I'm going. Would you like to walk with me?"

"Sure." Then I extended my hand and introduced myself, "I'm John from Tiberias."

Likewise, he extended his, "And I'm Andrew."

We walked together for several miles in our comfortable solitude before Andrew broke the silence. "John, forgive me for not visiting with you more, but my heart is heavy."

"What happened?"

"Do you really have the time to hear?"

"Sure go ahead."

"Well, it began three years ago as my brother, Peter, and I were mending our fishing nets. A man named Jesus stopped to talk. He had such a winsome demeanor that we both said 'yes' to His request to be His disciples."

"Did this mean you no longer fished?"

"No, fishing is our livelihood, but we have fished less because we wanted to spend as much time as possible with Jesus." Now Andrew raised his arm to point, "The larger house just ahead is where Peter lives. He moved there from Bethsaida. The house is large enough for his family and his wife's mother. I live alone in the small house next door. Since it is nearing supper time, would you like to come in and join me?"

"I'd like that very much."

When we arrived at the doorway, Andrew pushed aside a sheepskin drape. The thick adobe walls held the temperature of the cool night throughout the day. As Andrew prepared our meal of dried fish, figs, bread, and wine, I noticed that he was shorter than I, but more muscular with powerful, calloused hands. Even though our acquaintance had begun only a few hours earlier, I already felt we were good friends.

Andrew motioned as he spoke, "John, you may sit on this mat."

He broke a loaf of bread and handed me one half of the loaf along with a cup of wine. There was something about sharing a meal that put us both at ease.

"Andrew, tell me more about your friend Jesus."

"He spent much of His time healing and teaching the people, but He spent even more of His time teaching His twelve disciples. He must have wondered if we would ever learn."

"What makes you say that?"

"Jesus told us He would have to die and that He would rise from the dead on the third day. But we just didn't get it."

"So He did die?"

"Yes, the week before last."

"You must be very sad."

"John, it's hard to explain, but He told us if we had faith in Him that we would make it through the difficult times. This is one of those times."

Outside it was getting harder and harder to distinguish the outline of trees from the back drop of the sea. Inside Andrew lit an olive-oil lamp. The shadow of his frame leaned forward as he continued. "Jesus had the power to heal the sick. Those healed told others, so every day people came from all around to be healed."

"How did He heal?"

"Sometimes He just spoke. At other times He required them to do something. For one blind man, He spit in the dust and placed the mud on the man's eyes."

"Was he able to see?"

"At first people were as trees walking, but then he could see clearly. Another thing, you should have heard Him teaching in the synagogues. One time He told the Pharisees how they had missed the whole point of God's instructions."

"I bet they were a little upset."

"A little upset? It wasn't long after that that they decided to kill Him!"

"I can see you are a man of faith to have weathered the death of your friend so well."

"John, would you like to go fishing with Peter and me tonight? We had planned to head out around midnight."

"Will you have room for me?"

"Sure, some can fish from our boat and the others from James' and John's. Why don't you lay down on this mat and get a few hours of sleep."

So I rolled out the mat then laid down on my back, staring at the shadows made by the moon shining through the open doorway. Soon I was sleeping.

It seemed like only moments had passed when I was awakened by a loud, jovial voice, "All good fishermen arise!"

A more familiar voice, that of Andrew, said, "Peter, this is my friend John. He would like to fish with us."

"Welcome aboard, John. You can take the place of the scoundrel that betrayed our Lord. Luckily for him he took his own life, for had he not, I might have."

"Remember Peter, Jesus taught us to forgive, even Judas."

"True, still I am mighty angry about it all."

And with that, we gathered up our gear and walked briskly toward the sea. At the shore, Peter, Thomas, Andrew, and I boarded one boat, and James,

John, Nathanael, and another disciple pushed off in the other. The disciples had good reason to be sad. I wondered if Peter had decided they should go fishing to get their minds off of their troubles. He definitely was the leader.

Peter stood in the front of the boat looking back at the shoreline to his left and then cast a heavenward glance at Polaris to the right. He seemed to be using landmarks to locate the spot on the open water where they had found fish before. After a while he called out to James and John, "Let's try it here."

Immediately the nets were lowered, and the men took up their oars. Most were stripped to the waist even though the night air was cold. The rowing and pulling in of the net flowed smoothly. When we found no fish in the net, we let it down again, and the sequence was patiently repeated.

Eventually, Andrew handed me the net, and since I had watched every move he had made, I was a ready hand. After several hours, I was cold, tired, and hungry. I could not recall having done such strenuous work in a long time. We were all getting discouraged when our nets kept coming up empty. Peter was ready to quit, but Andrew convinced him to try a few more times.

Then at the first sign of dawn, Peter yelled across to James and John, "Let's take her in boys!"

As we approached land, we could see smoke curling straight up from a camp fire on the shore about a quarter of a mile away. Beside the fire was the figure of a man.

As we closed the distance, the man on the shore called out, "Did you catch any fish?"

ANDREW: THE FRIENDLIEST DISCIPLE

Peter spoke for all of us, "Nothing for this night's effort."

Then came back the response, "Throw out your net on the right-hand side of the boat, and you'll get plenty of them."

We all looked at each other, then Thomas stated the question we were all asking, "Why throw the net here? You can't catch fish in the shallows."

But Andrew, without a word, threw the net over the right-hand side of the boat. Soon it was overflowing with fish, and we all strained to pull the net into the boat, but were not able. John, now recognizing the man, said, "Peter, it is our Lord."

Without another thought, Peter wrapped his outer garment around his waist and threw himself into the sea. I turned to Andrew to say, "Peter certainly has a rambunctious love for Jesus."

The rest of us came in the boat dragging the net full of fish. By now, even Thomas was convinced that the man was Jesus. When we reached the shore, Peter helped us draw the net to land. I could see some fish on a fire of coals. Jesus said, "Bring some of the fish you have caught."

Immediately Peter spoke directly to each disciple assigning tasks for preparation of the fish. While Thomas was emptying the net, he counted one hundred and fifty-three fish and remarked with amazement that he could not find even one tear in the net. It wasn't long before the fish had been cooked over the fire.

Jesus turned to us and said, "Come and have breakfast."

Jesus, carrying bread, hot fish, and wine walked towards me. His servant attitude made me think of Him as a friend rather than a Messiah.

Then He read my thoughts, saying, "John, I know you must be famished after a night of fishing. Take this bread and fish and wine to nourish your body."

I shall never forget those eyes that looked into mine with such a caring spirit. As I accepted the food, I noticed that in the center of each of His calloused hands was a recent wound. It was almost as if each had been pierced by a large nail.

Then Jesus served Andrew, and moved on to another. As Jesus turned away, I leaned toward Andrew and said, "You told me Jesus was the Messiah. Why would a Messiah serve me?"

"More than a Messiah, He is a servant. That is the way He leads. He said for us to learn from His example."

The sun was fully up now, and my father would be wondering what had happened to me, so I turned to Andrew and said, "I must be going now. Thank you so much for your hospitality. After I deliver a payment to customs, I will return to Tiberias and tell all my friends about Jesus the Messiah."

Based on John 21:1-14.

Bartholomew:
The Innkeeper with Compassion

*M*y name is Bartholomew. My wife Abigail and I have been innkeepers in Bethlehem for sixty years. Today a distinguished physician named Luke took a room at our inn and asked if my wife and I would join him for supper.

Abigail runs the kitchen, I take care of the rooms, and our adoptive daughter Amaris serves the meals to the guests. For tonight's meal Abigail prepared her favorite mutton stew then joined Luke and me at the corner table in the dining area.

After Abigail was seated, Luke said, "They tell me this is the inn where Jesus was born. Is that true?"

"Yes, but why do you ask about that miraculous birth of sixty years ago?"

"I am traveling across Judea, Samaria, and Galilee talking with eyewitnesses of the events of Jesus' life to write an account for Theophilus. Do you remember Jesus' birth?"

"Oh, yes, as if it were only yesterday. Joseph asked for a room for his wife. Of course at the time, the inn was already filled with travelers coming to register for the Roman census."

"But if you were full, how was it that the family stayed here?"

"As I was turning Joseph away, Abigail walked past me to the young woman saying, 'Why, you are heavy with child and appear tired. Your husband can make you a bed in the covered stable behind the inn. He will find plenty of clean straw.'"

"So they spent the winter night in your stable?"

Abigail's expression was radiant as she spoke, "The young mother-to-be told me her name was Mary and that she and Joseph had traveled from Nazareth in Galilee. Joseph was a large man. His hands bore heavy calluses. Mary looked small beside her powerful husband but was strong in her own right. Once they had decided to stay, I loaned Joseph two sheepskin covers and Mary several cotton cloths, for she looked ready to give birth."

"Was Mary's baby born that night?"

"Yes, but she wasn't alone. Shortly after dusk Abigail and I were awakened by footsteps outside our window. When we looked to see who it was, we saw a group of shepherds moving toward the stable so we decided to join them. When we got to the stable, the shepherds knelt down around the baby who was wrapped in cotton cloths and lying in the manger. There was a radiance beaming out from the baby and the mother."

"Why did the shepherds come?"

"One of the shepherds told me they had been tending their flocks when an angel of the Lord suddenly stood before them saying, 'Do not be afraid, for I bring you good news of a great joy for a baby has been born in Bethlehem, for you a Savior, who is Christ the Lord. You will find Him wrapped in cloths and lying in a manger.'"

The olive oil in the lamp on the table was getting low, and all the other guests had retired to their rooms. The hour was late and Luke, Abigail, and I had lost track of time as we discussed Jesus' birth. By this time, Amaris had joined us at the table after cleaning up the kitchen.

"Have you told me all you know about the life of Jesus?"

"There is more about the day Jesus was crucified. Amaris and her husband Judd and their young sons, David and Zared, were staying in our stable the week before the crucifixion. Judd had been harshly accused of stealing some vegetables in the market, and he and another robber were crucified on either side of Jesus. Amaris has remained with us like a daughter, and David and Zared now have families of their own."

Amaris' face and hair were damp from her work in the kitchen, so she dabbed her face with her apron before leaning forward into the light of the olive oil lamp. Amaris had a beautiful face and an even more beautiful spirit. The three of us could tell she wanted to speak, so we waited.

Shyly she began, "Judd was not a bad man. He took some food for us, his hungry family. Even though he died a cruel death, I have a peace, knowing Jesus, and having been told His words on the cross for Judd were, 'Truly I say to you, today you shall be with me in paradise.' As a follower of Jesus, I know that I too shall be reunited with Judd in heaven some day."

Abigail, with tears welling up in her eyes, reached out for Amaris' hands. Luke placed his hands on top of theirs. Then I placed my hands on his. Amaris bowed her head and quietly thanked the Lord for His goodness and for bring-

124

ing Luke our way. The silent moment following her prayer only served to draw us closer, then I said, "Amen." And everyone else said, "Amen."

With that we lifted our heads only to find that there wasn't a dry eye among us. Luke began to gather his notes and thanked us for our time as it was getting well into the evening hours. Amaris picked up the dishes while Abigail brushed the crumbs off of the table and I pushed in the chairs. All was quiet when I picked up the lamp and guided everyone to their rooms.

Based on Luke 1:1-4, 2:1-20, 23:39-43.

Other Penbrooke Books You Will Enjoy:

Love Letters To Remember (ISBN # 1-889116-02-5)

Letters to Mother (ISBN # 1-889116-00-9)

Joy of Christmas (ISBN # 1-889116-09-2)

Sister of Mine (ISBN # 1-889116-08-4)

Everlasting Friendship (ISBN # 1-889116-04-1)

Significant Acts of Kindness (ISBN # 1-889116-01-7)

The Little Book of Happies (ISBN # 1-889116-03-3)

A Timeless Gift of Love (ISBN # 1-889116-05-X)

My False Teeth Fit Fine, But I Sure Miss My Mind (ISBN # 1-889116-07-6)

A Tribute to Mom (ISBN # 1-889116-12-2)

A Tribute to Dad (ISBN # 1-889116-13-0)

PENBROOKE
PUBLISHING

P. O. Box 700566 · Tulsa, OK 74170